The Monk, the Mushroom, and the MRI
Dan Holloway

Books in the Creative Living series

Living in Longhand (2023)
The Monk, the Mushroom, and the MRI (2024)

The Creative Living series also includes the creative thinking card game Mycelium, and a series of infographic cards and guides that accompany the techniques outlined in this book. You can explore the full range at rogueinterrobang.com

© Dan Holloway 2024, all rights reserved

Published by Rogue Interrobang Press

An imprint of Rogue Interrobang Limited, Company number 11730049. Registered address: c/o Woodstock Accountancy 3aMarketPlace, Woodstock, Oxfordshire, OX20 1SY

Cover design by JD Smith Design Ltd

You can sign up for our creative newsletter by scanning the QR code below. We will be in touch from time to time with tips, challenges, curiosities, and (very occasionally) to tell you about our new books and games.

Contents

Preface	7
Introduction	9
A note on exercises in this book	10
What is creativity?	12
Exercise 1: What does creativity mean to you?	12
AI and creativity	15
Defining Creativity	19
Doing New Things	23
Creativity as a Soft Skill	25
A Note on the Structure of This Book	28
Learn lots of things about lots of things	33
Creativity Isn't (only) What You Know, It's How You Know It	33
Exercise 2: What do you Know?	34
Everything in Its Right Place?	36
Exercise 3: "Just So" Stories	38
Learn About Lots of Things	41
Building your Knowledge Map	41
Exercise 4: An Archive of Your Own	48
Broad Learning or Deep Learning?	50
Exercise 5: What problem do you want to solve?	52
Don't Learn Things Because You Think They Will Be Useful	57
Points, lines, and systems: understanding a problem	59

Exercise 6: Disentangling Problems	64
Set the Problem Aside and Start Learning	65
Learn about what interests you. But don't "follow your passion"	66
A Pin in the Page	67
Preparing the Page	71
Exercise 7: Preparing a List to Choose From	72
Learn Lots About Each Thing	73
Learn Like a Detective: Interrogate The Subject	76
10 "Key" Questions to Unlock a Subject	78
Exercise 8: Interrogating the Subject	78
Creative questions in depth	80
Exercise 9: Further Enquiries	91
Learning Things to Use Them Not to Store Them: The Power of Projects	93
A Portfolio of Projects	93
A Variation on Parallel Projects: Reading Two (or more) Books at Once	96
Exercise 10: Reading Together	100
Effective reading for creativity	101
Techniques for Managing Your Project Portfolio	105
Resource Specific Task Lists	105
Project Management	107
Commonplace Book	111
Zettelkasten	115
Value Extraction	118

Exercise 11: The Value of Anything	121
Building a Palace for the Mind	122
From Cabbies to Nobel Prizes: the Neuroscience of Creativity (Part 1)	125
An Explanation and Short but Colourful Edited History of the "Method of Loci"?	132
Building Your Own Palace of the Mind	137
Creating the architecture	138
Using (all) your senses	141
Movement and Exaggeration	144
Familiarity and Order	146
Exercise 12: Build your own mind palace.	147
Joining the Dots	148
All that jazz: The Neuroscience of Creativity (Part 2)	148
Deliberate Practice	151
Learning to Turn Off Your Self-Censor	153
Mycelium: new connections	156
How it works	158
Exercise 13: Icy ants	161
Taking Ideas for a Walk	165
Context, Constraint, and Creativity	167
Mental hooks	170
Mental imagery	172
Exercise 14: Walking the Dog	181
Living Creatively	184

Creative walking	186
Observing and questioning	188
Play	190
Combine things that aren't usually combined	193
Acknowledgements	196

Preface

I have written many books over the years on many subjects, from thrillers to magical realism; poetry to advice on the publishing process; young adult fantasy to powerlifting. While I'm what writers would call a "pantser" (I don't ever start out with a fully formed map of where I'm going, just a starting point, an idea of where I'm going, and curiosity as to how I'll get there), in decades I've been writing, I've developed what would come close to meeting the description of a system. And it serves me pretty well. It takes me 2 to 3 months to write, and the same to edit, a book; a month to recharge the batteries; a month to immerse myself in the world of a new book; and then the same cycle. Regardless of the subject or genre.

Creativity is the thing I know best in the world. I have been competing at the Creative Thinking World Championship since its inception in 1997, and contributed to Bill Hartston's creativity column for years before that. I have been immersed in the creative process for well over four and a half of my five decades. And, also in 1997, I started researching the way people have thought about what it means to be creative over almost three millennia. I have devised a creative thinking game, won awards for creativity tools as well as 4 Creative Thinking World Championships, and founded a start-up dedicated to the subject.

But any attempt to write more about creativity than a workshop, an article, the rule booklet for a game, or some interleaved thoughts in a memoir has proven utterly in vain for the many years I have been trying to do so.

I've contemplated many possible reasons for this failure as I have stubbornly insisted on continuing to figure out a way into a book like this.

Is the problem that for once I always seem to find myself trying to plot out a structure in advance and my brain simply can't handle the dissonance of that?

Is it because I'm too close to the subject to understand what it is like to come at it with a fresh mind?

Is it something more sinister? An unshakeable awareness of the fast approaching shadow of AI that, far from making creativity stand out as our uniquely human asset, may well make it one of the first aspects of being human to be truly replaceable?

Determining, finally, to write this book (largely because when I started I had the manuscripts of the book before it and the book after it complete, neither of which make any real sense without this as the filling!) felt like an act of pure but doomed will. Believing it was completable made me feel like the Queen of Hearts proclaiming one more impossible thing believed before breakfast.

But breakfast feels like an age ago. Since then I have run a half marathon along the Ridgeway, finished reading a fascinating account of the history of hacking[1], eaten three more meals and counting, and put the last full stop on the final page of this book. The heart of Wonderland is believing impossible things. And the heart of creativity is finding out whether or not you can make them happen.

[1] Nicola Perlroth, *This is How They Tell Me the World Ends*, Bloomsbury 2021.

Introduction

There are many skills that can help you do things better, make the world a better place in very particular ways. Plumbing, or programming Javascript, or nurturing saplings into hardy mature trees for example. And there are other skills that enable you to deploy them. To decide where plumbing in sanitation will save most lives; or which projects to greenlight a team of Javascript programmers to build; to evaluate which forests are in greatest need of regrowth; or to weigh up all options and decide that the best thing to do with the next 20 years of your life is to learn how to build things out of graphene.

If you want to make the most impact on the world, you need to develop as many of that second type of skill as you possibly can. Their breadth will give you the ability to be resilient and flexible, to be able to make an important contribution whatever unexpected direction the world might take. Examples of such skills are critical reading, mental modelling, critical thinking, logical reasoning, engaging an audience through empathy. Communication.

And creativity.

Creativity is a fundamental skill in the sense that you can build whole towers of knowledge, problem-solving, education, influence, and hope upon it.

It's the most urgent of these skills because we all need it. Whether you are a brand struggling to convey a message to your audience about how you can change their lives; an institution or think tank working on the most fundamental problems facing humanity; a research hub pushing the boundaries of science, unsure where the results will lead you; or just a disillusioned 50-something lying awake at night looking out of the window at the stars and wondering why, when you were a kid, you would have stared in awe and hope at that same night sky and imagined yourself going there one day and now all you see is an annoying background light that's doing nothing for your insomnia—what all of those have in common is that they are in some way stuck. Stuck because they cannot imagine a future outside the tram tracks of the past.

Creativity is the raw material of that imagination.

And it's the most important skill because it's something taught out of many of us as we grow. The kid who gazes in wonder at the stars doesn't become the 50 year old insomniac because that's the natural way of things. That curiosity is taught out of them by school, by society, by a family who wants them to go the way of their predecessors, by friends who want them to join in, by the collective gaze of neighbours making sure they fit the community brief, by bosses who value doing the same thing everyone else does but ever so slightly better.

But the good news is it can be taught back in.

This book will show you how.

A note on exercises in this book

This book contains a number of exercises, just as my workshops do. You can, of course, skip these, giving you more flexibility than you would have in a workshop. But you can use them in different ways to help you understand and enhance your creative progress. And of course you can revisit them as often as you would like.

If you want to follow the exercises in the order they appear in the book, you can do that in two different ways. Each brings its own benefits. You can prime your brain for the section you are about to cover in the book by doing the exercise before you start reading. Or you can reinforce what you have just learned by doing the exercise when you have finished (better still, the day after, to both refresh and reinforce what you have learned). Either approach works well. Doing both also works. Just go with whatever works best for you.

For each exercise, I will provide a short commentary on how to think about the answers you have given. I thought about putting these at the back of the book so you could avoid looking at them in advance like you would a school arithmetic book. But instead I have included them in the text. That way, if you decide not to do the exercises, you can still gain something from the accompanying text without the distraction of page flipping. I am also a great believer in the importance of brain priming. So if you catch glimpses of post exercise thought before you begin I think that will enhance not detract from the exercise itself.

A final point. And this one really matters, so remember it well. This is a book about creativity. There aren't right answers. There are interesting rabbit holes to go down. There are interesting thoughts to play with, interesting questions to ask, and interesting insights to incorporate into your journey through this book and through your creative life.

What is creativity?

Having said everything I did in that introduction, what better way to start than with an exercise. It's a very simple one. But not necessarily a very easy one. A tension you will discover at every turn as you unpeel the many layers of the creative process.

Exercise 1: What does creativity mean to you?

This is the first question I ask any person or any group that works with me. And it's the first thing I'm asking you.

Your answer to this question will, quite probably, be the reason you bought this book.

There is no right answer, just like most questions. But as is also the case with most of the questions here, it matters that you are able to pin down your own thoughts. Because doing that will help you get the most from what follows.

It may help you to break the question down into the following parts (hint: most questions are not actually single questions. And the confusion we often feel when trying to answer them often comes from falsely assuming they are. It almost always helps to try to break questions down into their fundamental parts):

- What would you be able to do if you were more creative that you can't do now?"
- What is the most important thing you want to achieve, that you haven't yet achieved because you think you need to be more creative?

And of course there is a related question:

- How would doing the thing you would be able to do if you were more creative enable you to achieve the thing you want to achieve?

Give yourself plenty of time.

Having done so, consider these further points. This is how I help people I work with break down something that can feel quite abstract. Worse still, thinking about what you want creativity to do in your life can feel quite daunting. The following can make it seem more manageable.

Often, the desire to be more creative can come from realising that something is missing from your toolbox. And that creativity is the thing that would fill the gap. Consider each of these things. If you feel as though you are missing any one, or combination, of them, that could explain why it is that the thing you most want to achieve has so far eluded you.

Of course, there may be many more absences outside of this list that stand between you and your goals. But these are the gaps that creativity can help you fill. And it will often be the case that one or a combination of these will be the key ingredient in overcoming many of the other obstacles as well.

Ask yourself if you feel any of these.

- A lack of invention (not enough original ideas)
- A lack of imagination (a lack of empathy/perspective)
- A lack of innovation (not enough relevant ideas)
- A lack of implementation (an inability to convert ideas to actions)
- A lack of impact (an inability to change the world when you do have a great idea)
- A lack of curiosity (not spending time looking for any/all of the above)
- A lack of communication (not telling people about your ideas)

- A lack of listening (not recognizing the significance of ideas you have already had)

Keep your answers as a working document. Return to it as you work through this book and others in this series. Whatever it is you have defined as creativity here will give shape to the rest of what you learn. It will help you understand what you are looking to this book to do, and that will help you to interrogate what I have written and the exercises you undertake to make sure they are working for you.

As you go, make a note of the spaces in your toolkit that have filled in. Maybe you could represent this visually, colouring in a chart or a map or an actual representation of a toolbox. You could even build yourself a structure out of Lego and add bricks as you progress through the book.

This will also keep you directed, heading towards the thing you most want. And it will motivate you, because it establishes a personal connection to what you are learning.

AI and creativity

I started writing this book in early 2022. During the first round of edits later that year, I confined the elephant in the room to a single paragraph:

"And during the course of writing this book, artificial intelligence has got so much better at so many tasks we traditionally associate with human creativity, that creative artists have started to worry what their role in the future might be; and some of us have started reflecting on whether we might have to change our definition of what creativity is— or at the very least whether we continue to think of it as something uniquely human."

As I get ready to publish in 2024, that solitary paragraph no longer adequate. The nuanced relationship between humans, machines, and the processes of creativity has grown ever more complex.

And of course, the sheer technical level of progress defies prediction. Even since starting this final round of edits a fortnight ago, we have seen the release of OpenAI's breathtaking text to video platform Sora, I have ceased any attempt to prognosticate. That way lies an endless loop of update and correction that is more an enemy of publishing what is good enough than the writer's traditional enemy of perfectionism.

New fields of activity and employment such as prompt engineering have sprung up as others seem to teeter on the edge of a cliff.

Amidst all this activity, speculation has intensified over the value of human effort in the creative process. Nowhere has this been more evident than the struggles of the world's legal frameworks to make sense of copyright laws designed for what feels like not just a past age but a past understanding. Traditionally copyright has protected the expression of creative ideas. The digital age was already making that concept, expression, which in an era of print and manufacture seemed so obvious, creak. AI has tied creators and legislators and tech companies alike in knots. What exactly are creative ideas? Whose ideas? And if they are ideas that originate from humans, then which human's ideas? The human who prompts the AI? The humans on whose work an AI is trained?

And beyond this is a level of even more uncomfortable questions. Which is more creative: the plagiarising human or the innovative algorithm?

And behind everything, as is so often the case with disruptive technologies, lies a question that has kept us awake at night for millennia. What does it mean to be human? Are we unique? Even as technology enables telescopes like James Webb to bring us images from the furthest edges of the universe, the question we have so often asked as we gazed up at the skies, "Are we alone in that vast seemingly empty space?" has been turned on its head and in on itself: "Are we alone on this tiny, crowded, claustrophobic sphere we have already pushed to an extreme where it can barely sustain one creative species?"

Taking us back to the question of human creativity, the head of the Association of American Publishers, Maria Pallante, asked bluntly at their 2023 AGM:

"Do we as a society want AI-generated works flooding the Internet, potentially depressing the value of human authorship?"

Creativity has often been defended as a last bastion of humanity in the face of the machines. But one development after another has made it clear that even when it comes to "soft skills," machines are getting very good very quickly.

So where does this leave us?

First, I will say that I haven't rewritten or restructured the vast majority of this book. I haven't changed my working definition of creativity, even as it slowly becomes a definition we are learning to share. After all, books on chess are still written as the game continues to fire the imagination long after Deep Blue's conquest over Kasparov. And the realisation there were cheetahs who would always outrun us, gorillas who could outpunch us, elephants who could outlift us, has done nothing to dent the growth of the fitness industry. Our fascination with, reward from, and desire to pursue creativity is no more threatened by AI than any of these other pursuits and will not be so long after our potential as humans has been outstripped by others.

And for the time being at least creativity retains an essential role beyond development and self-fulfilment, in the challenge to which it has so far been uniquely suited: finding a solution to those problems whose root is human habit, bias, convention, and herd behaviour.

Creativity does one thing machines do exceptionally well. It combines existing ideas into new ones. This is something it remains as important as ever for humans to do. Because it provides a sense check on the machines. Because doing it is a fundamental part of fulfilling our human performance potential, as much as running or lifting. And because it is such a fundamental mental exercise that practising it improves a myriad other skills, and training it rigorously and in the right ways has the power to change the make upland operation of our brain itself, with every added benefit that brings.

And there are two elements of creativity I will touch on in this book: the extent to, and time for, which they elude machines is something I am not arrogant or foolish enough to speculate upon.

First is the possibility of what those who work in the neuroscience of the field call "a-ha" moments. Long though a myth, the instant spark of insight turns out to have a neurological correlate that differentiates it from other forms of processing, synthesizing, or learning. In practical terms we might think of this as the potential to produce ideas that aren't quite so limited by the garbage in garbage out constraints of dataset-trained machine learning. AI is dependent on the sources used to train it. In particular it is hard to configure its outputs so they become aware of and push against the biases inherent in those training data. AI is, as AlphaGo famously demonstrated, capable of surprising, even startling, a human observer. Whether that surprise would extend to a human who was also trained on the same dataset remains unclear. But the human mind does, for now, seem capable of doing surprising and, crucially, counter-intuitive and even counter-evidential things with its experience. Nurturing that trait remains, for now, not just the part of fostering our potential it will always be but a crucial step in helping us to find ways out of the problematic trains of thought and action that lie behind our gravest challenges.

And second, while AI is marvellous at combining existing ideas into new ones, for now (can we take it as read that I am appending these statements with "for now?") it remains less good at telling us the relative value of the ideas it spits out. That is, it is great at the generation of ideas. Lots of ideas. But less good at selection from those ideas. Especially when it comes to evaluating which ideas might solve problems whose cause lies in the dataset that generated the ideas. By which I mean, if we take a challenge like climate change, we might be able to feed lots of information about human behaviour into a system to generate possible solutions. But if we now ask which of those solutions we should pursue, anything trained on human behaviour will be unable to see outside the limitations that caused the problem in the first place.

What we really need if we are to solve our great challenges is a way of selecting between the ideas we generate that understands the foibles of human nature in a way that will enable the chosen idea to be practical while being distant enough from those same foibles to avoid falling into the assumptions that have so far stopped us solving the problem.

This book will take us through not just the generation of ideas, but ways to nudge and nurture the possibility of surprise. A large part of the next book in this series will focus on this second "selection and implementation" conundrum.

Defining Creativity

So, with that very long-winded series of caveats and qualifications out of the way, let's go back to where we started.

What is creativity?

For many it is related to art and artistic expression in all its forms. The debates around AI have shown how entrenched this way of thinking has become over the centuries. Whether the art in question involves a brush, a pen, a voice, or a keyboard, what makes it "creative" is that it begins with some uniquely human blend of invention and intention of which the "work of art" is the expression.

It is this artistic ideal of creativity we perhaps think of when we associate the creative process with people touched by what we might think of as "genius." This is the creativity of those who are somehow different, whether they are born that way or simply, in the words of Apple's legendary ad campaign, "are crazy enough to think they can change the world." It is creativity as "a-ha moment." This is a theory that has fallen very much out of fashion as the communal has replaced the individual as the seat of what it truly means to be human in the public consciousness. But it is a theory that some neuroscientists have recently, tentatively started to pluck pieces of from the garbage bin of ideas.

In contrast to this, one could argue that creativity is not what happens when you get gifted individuals, but something that emerges from the combined efforts of vast numbers. In this way of thinking it is what we might call "an emergent property" of a concerted effort to find a solution to a problem. It's almost a numbers game. On the one hand, the more people you have working on the same problem, the more likely it is that somewhere you will get an outlier of an idea that has wings. On the other hand, having lots of people thinking and talking together creates a vast number of interconnections that builds a system so large and complex that sometimes it reaches a threshold where something interesting bubbles up.

James Kaufman and Ronald Beghetto's Four C Model of creativity[2] builds on the sense that creativity can mean several things according to the level at which it takes place and, crucially, the sphere in which the result of a creative process is really unique. Such models assume there is something similar about the creativity we engage in every day and the creativity of great artists and inventors. But also that there is something that makes the two things distinct.

The fours Cs (mini, little, Pro, and Big) start with a child or grown-up doing something for the very first time (something billions of other people have done and will do, but is a new activity to them), and progresses through acquiring a skill or achieving a personal best (a new level of attainment with an area you are already familiar with), to making a breakthrough within a field of interest or profession, and ultimately doing something within a field that changes the world. This is a story of creativity where increased impact and innovation work (largely) in lockstep with increased expertise.

In contrast, the most viewed TED talk of all time, Ken Robinson's "Do Schools Kill Creativity"[3], has lent weight to a popular line of thought that runs counter to this. Robinson argues that children are great at creativity and become slowly worse at it as overly-structured education teaches them step by step to avoid the very things that make up curiosity: play, curiosity, questioning, what one might call a mischievous disregard for convention.

Having spent years running public engagement events in which I give creative thinking exercises to adults and children together, I have a lot of time for Ken Robinson's ideas. I don't

---

[2] https://journals.sagepub.com/doi/10.1037/a0013688
[3] https://www.youtube.com/watch?v=iG9CE55wbtY

The Monk, The Mushroom, and the MRI

think I can remember a parent ever producing a more creative set of answers than their child.

Like an annoying teacher who sets a test to which history has provided multiple possible answers, I will conclude that there is something to be said for each of these theories.

Possibly what is most valuable about understanding each of them is not whether it is true, but how it would affect your approach to creativity if it were true. Leaving aside the "lone genius" for now, believing that collaboration and discussion of ideas can help; that building expertise is valuable; and that retaining or rediscovering a sense of curiosity and questioning are essential pursuits—all of these will greatly help you develop a more creative life.

And while the idea that some people just are and some people just aren't creative serves little useful purpose (and many harmful ones such as the perennial I'm not creative" plea that has become a cliché in TED talks but which experience has taught me all too often is one of the strongest beliefs people have about themselves), one can flip the theory so that it has value. What it can teach us is that our original ideas are important, no matter how ridiculous they seem, no matter the letters we have after our name or the job title we have been given. And they are worth holding onto, exploring, testing. If we take from the "inspired person" model of creativity the notion that world-changing ideas can be found in unexpected places, then we might learn to hold onto and pursue our ideas until experience and experiment, rather than an "expert", dismisses them.

But for the purposes of this book I'm not proposing a theory. Or a complex definition. I'm not setting one ideology, one strand of history or set of data against another. I'm proposing something simple and practical. I will focus on the definition I find most useful, because pursuing it will help you develop a skill that you can use to change the world (whether that's the little-c world of your family life or the Big-C world). If you don't want to call that skill creativity, that's fine. You may be right. But learn it anyway.

Over the course of this book, and the books that precede and follow it, I will show you the practical ways in which you can use this newly acquired skill to build the change you want to see in the world in which you want to see it.

So what is this definition of creativity? Does it live up to that length and level of drumroll? Hardly. Creativity, as we will learn about it here, means:

doing new things.

Doing New Things

Creativity is simply bringing new things into the world.

It sounds like an anticlimax.

It isn't.

What exactly are the new things creativity brings into being? The new things creative people do?

As you may have guessed, they are at least as many as the definitions of creativity we just listed. But whichever of those definitions you want to run with; whatever it is that, to go back to our earlier thought experiment, you personally want from being more creative, it will involve new things.

Those new things might, in the most common sense of creativity, be objects: paintings or poems; sculptures, buildings, exquisite pieces of design. They might be strategies to solve knotty personal problems: which set of feuding in-laws to spend the holidays with, how to make school lunches more interesting, how to fit all the books of a newly discovered author on non-existent shelf space. They might be actions or processes: a new sport, a new way of generating electricity, a more efficient way of painting cars on a production line. Or they could be ideas that uproot centuries of history by turning our world on its head: like evolution by natural selection, or the belief that some rights might belong to every living being for no other reason than that they are alive.

I say this is the most useful definition of creativity because it gets to the heart of another question. Why should we care about creativity? Why should we dedicate time and resources to creativity when there are so many pressing problems in the world competing for our attention?

The answer is simple: because it is only with creativity that we can truly hope to solve the problems that matter most to us. So many of the world's problems, or on a smaller level our own, come from the way we think and act right now. From processes that worked once upon a time and have slowly rusted away ever since. It is newness that promises hope in the face of all these seemingly insoluble problems. And creativity is the art, or rather the skill, the technique, of the new. It is the one skill on which all the other skills we need in order to make the world better depend. And as such it demands the investment of our time.

Creativity as a Soft Skill

This is precisely what people mean when they talk about creativity as a "soft skill" or "transferable skill" or "general skill". These are simply terms to describe skills on which other skills are built. In this way, creativity is like doing the deadlift or squat in the gym. Unless you are a competitive powerlifter (or, as some of us are misguided enough to be, a competitive creative thinker), there are very few physical activities that require you to squat or to deadlift. But there is a vast array of physical activity that depends upon the muscle and ligament strength, the range of motion, the explosive power that squatting and deadlift build.

Creativity in its purest form is very like this. You will spend very little time in life thinking of weird and wonderful uses for a paperclip, or similarities between a cabbage and a fire engine. But spending time using exercises like that to train your mental muscles will fit you very well for a whole host of challenges you face every single day.

Soft skills like this are part of a fundamental infrastructure that we need to build in order to flourish and attain our dreams.

A helpful way to understand how creativity functions as a soft skill is to think of a problem you might imagine someone facing in the not too distant future.

Suppose you were on the crew of the first human flight to Mars. Suppose you were told there was a flaw in the design of the ship leaving only enough room for you to take one tool with you.

What would you take? You could take a screwdriver, but what if you got to Mars to find you really needed a drill. You could take a drill but what if you got there to find you really needed a spanner? And so on. The answer, of course, is that you take a 3D printer. Now whatever problem you find when you get there you can print the right tool for the job.

Solving our most important problems is very much like trying to reach Mars in this sense. There are lots of skills you could learn, but most of them will only help you with some parts of some problems, and we never really know in advance which specific setbacks and challenges we are going to face when we first set out to take on a problem. Creativity is the mental equivalent of a 3D printer. Whatever you come up against, creativity will give your brain the best shot at finding a way over, around, or straight through it.

As we'll see later, creativity works like this because it prepares your brain to be flexible, to think fluidly. This is not just a metaphor. There is some evidence from neuroscience that the brains of people who are more creative actually have a different structure. And not a structure that is different from birth, but one that changes as a result of specific training.

Creative brains can have more actual matter, more connections, and more activity in some areas: the areas associated with stitching ideas and knowledge together in new ways.

And they find it easier to overcome our inhibitions to form new ideas.

Because of the brain's remarkable neuroplasticity (its ability to change structure as it adapts to new stimuli) many people can induce these changes in the structure of their brains by training. Many of the exercises in this book have been designed to provide exactly this kind of training stimulus.

These two qualities of creative brains (high levels of idea-storing-and-forming stuff, and low inhibition to trying new things) reflect two fundamental ingredients of creativity. These ingredients are, respectively, the raw materials that allow us to do new things, and the process by which manipulation of those raw materials leads to the production of those new things.

We will spend most of this book acquainting ourselves with, and learning how to develop, these two magic ingredients. They are:

- An extensive knowledge of a large number of things;

and

- The ability to connect those things fluidly.

We will start out by learning how to learn more, and how to learn it really efficiently so that, like high grade rocket fuel, it's able to be readily deployed, and with little effort or waste turned into creative outputs.

Then we will focus on how to get really good at manipulating all that raw material into exciting, surprising, useful, delightful new things.

Training those two elements of creativity will also involve literally training your brain. It may change its actual physical structure. It will certainly make it more efficient at being creative.

Follow the techniques outlined in this book and you will have succeeded in equipping yourself with the best possible toolkit to solve every other challenge that comes your way.

A Note on the Structure of This Book

The problem with books can be that they are the verbal equivalent of a painting. But it can so often feel that what you need as a writer is something that equates to a sculpture. Wouldn't it be incredible if words worked could be written, and read, in three dimensions?

It was this possibility that first made me excited about the possibilities that writing online might offer. Mightn't hyperlinks be a way of structuring words so that you could read, and write, both side to side and bottom to top so to speak? To pursue information on one axis or another?

As a child my favourite reading experiences approximated to this in some ways, and I feel as though I have been chasing the magic of that process of mental exploration ever since.

Two things I loved as a child were stamps and library sales.

When I was about 7 or 8 I started staying with my grandmother on my own for a week or so at a time. I didn't realise at the time this was because my parents were trying to stop their marriage falling apart and needed me out of the way. I just thought I was going on an adventure to Bournemouth.

A strange set of characters passed through my gran's house. A reflection of the somewhat bohemian life she, and later on my mother, had led. One of those was a quiet, awkward, 50-something family friend whose passion in life was stamp collecting. When he came to visit he would show me through his collections and leave me with several huge carrier bags filled with random stamps from all over the world. Always completely unsorted. And always peppered with little seams of old and unusual finds that made it worth sorting through to the very end of every bag.

I would scatter the bags out on the floor of the room I was staying in and over the week piles would build as I sorted them painstakingly by country, by denomination, by what I thought from the look of them might be their age.

At the same time, our local library in Stroud had regular sales of the books it no longer needed. Almost always these were the kind of non-fiction books that got replaced every few years by new editions. And these included stamp catalogues. For 5p I could pick up an A4 sized catalogue of the stamps of the world that was well over a thousand pages long. It was several years out of date. But that didn't bother me. The thousands of stamps I had painstakingly arranged were years, decades, or over a century old.

My journey as a reader of stamp catalogues began in an attempt to sort the stamps I had by age. As I did so I learned the names of countries in their own language, I learned new alphabets. And I learned their history, often their politics as they moved from monarchy to republic, occupied to independent, single state to splintered satellites and vice versa.

But most of all I learned a new way to read. When I came across an event in one country from, say, 1965, I wanted to know how other countries had commemorated that event. So I put a finger as a marker and moved to another country. And as I moved through its pages I would do the same again. Soon my fingers were all occupied and I would turn the corners over. And I wouldn't sleep until I had finished and then retraced my steps back through all the pages that had led me on every tangent. I could lose myself in this endless cross-referencing for hours at a time, never tiring, learning more about the world and its myriad languages and images and the way everything meshed together than any textbook could ever have taught.

In the case of this book, the desire to write on two entirely different axes at the same time is a very practically-based one. And it goes back to the conundrum I posed in my preface. Why have I found it so hard over the years to write a book on a subject I know so well? The answer is that this single book needs to be two books. In one I explain the theory of creativity, its history, and the experiments that over the years have led to that theoretical understanding. At that point my reader feels on solid ground, confident they can navigate the territory, ready to step off the pavement onto the open rugged trail of practice. But they are also somewhat bored, and have settled into a passivity that makes taking such a step so much harder than it might otherwise be.

In a second version of the book, I do what I do with my workshops. I launch people into an exercise. I tease their brains. And only having done so, having familiarised them with the tools at their command, do I explain what the purpose of those exercises has been. Only then do I start to let that seething morass of mental muscle coalesce around a structure that will tame and direct it. But those readers are left confused and exhausted before they understand what it is they are exhausting themselves for. And whereas in a workshop I can exhort them to "trust the process" and provide assurance by my tone, my ad hoc anecdotes, my physical presence, that everything will be OK, a book can leave them cast adrift.

So the structure of this book is a necessary compromise.

We have identified two ingredients of creativity, and they need addressing in sequence. First, learning lots of things. Second, joining those things together.

And for each of those it is important to understand both theory and practice.

The structure I am following is to explain the theory and then the practice of each in turn. The structural trick I am using to justify keeping you waiting to understand what those initial exercises are for is to paint them with a generous wash of foreshadowing. Learning lots of things is not an end in itself. It is a tool to give us the raw materials which we can then join together. And to do that means learning in a particular way.

And in the second part, I hold things together by constantly encouraging you to join together what you have learned with a constant glance back over your shoulder. Creating new things from your raw materials, done properly, makes it easier to gather more raw materials, and so a virtuous cycle builds. One of learning, using, building, testing, finding holes and filling them, finding new uses for those filling materials, building more, and so on.

Learning is not just storing facts, but priming those facts so they are ready to be used in making new ideas that will have an impact on the world. And combining new ideas creatively is not just about burning through raw materials on some accelerationist sprint to the horizon. It's about creating new structures that will alter how we perceive the world, and deepen our future learning.

So each one of the two sections that follows will move from exercises to orient you in your new surrounding; to an explanation of why I have placed you here; to a tour of some of the experiments that have shaped our understanding of the territory (and an introduction to some of those who have stood there before); building to a set of tools to work with to explore that landscape.

But one thing never changes. This book is a tool to help you change the world in the ways that matter to you most. Whether that's a personal problem that's been sending you round and round in circles for years with no solution in sight;

or an existential challenge to humanity itself, born from the habits we humans just can't seem to shake.

Learn lots of things about lots of things

Creativity Isn't (only) What You Know, It's How You Know It

Knowledge is the raw material of creativity, just as the most fundamental particles of physics are the raw materials for the unfolding of and evolution within the natural world. The most complex, impactful, beautiful, enriching ideas we could ever create are all built from the very simplest, most basic mental building blocks it is possible to break an idea down into. They are so in exactly the same way a waterfall, or a palace, a revolution, a lifelong love affair, the glint of a peacock's tail in the sun, or the billions of stars that make up a galaxy are all built from the same unimaginably small units.

Not all combinations of those particles into physical materials are equally useful in building the wonders of the universe around us. The ones that aren't come and go leaving little impact except for fleeting traces. Likewise not all clusters of ideas are equally useful in creating the concepts, dreams, ambitions and solutions that transform our future. But if they do not form into clusters at all, we know they will have no real use.

We can, that is, decide by imagination and experiment which combinations of ideas, which connections, are useful for solving our problems at a later date. First we need to form those connections.

And to continue with our physical/chemical analogy, that means ensuring the things we know are not inert noble gases but rather highly reactive elements fizzing with anticipation of the compounds they might form.

We can express this in a simple principle:

To be creative, you don't learn things so that you can remember them. You learn things so you can use them.

To frame that in terms of knowledge, the principle would be

Knowledge needs to be easy to use, more than it needs to be easy to recall.

As we will see, this doesn't mean that memory doesn't matter. Or that a good memory is nothing more than a party trick. People hundreds, thousands even, of years ago who developed the memory techniques still used by memory athletes today understood this very well. For them memory and creativity were two sides of the same thing. They realised that both were fundamental to imagining a different future, a better future; to persuading others of the value of what they imagined; and to making the future they imagined a reality.

In this book, I want to show you how to use memory and creativity together in this way; how to turn ideas into the building blocks of imagination; and how to start the process of imagining a future that is different, one that is better than it would be if you simply allowed things to carry on as they are.

Exercise 2: What do you Know?

To start to appreciate how inseparable knowledge and creativity are, I want you really to think about what you know. Everything you know. What do you think of? If you are a visual thinker, how would you visualise it? If you are a conceptual thinker, how would you describe it?

It is easy to think of knowledge as a set of items in a basket, or on a list; or as a collection of objects in a filing cabinet, a museum, a catalogue or a zettelkasten (a card index, like many of us will have grown up with in libraries and teenagers are rediscovering on productivity YouTube).

The Monk, The Mushroom, and the MRI

This is the way of thinking about knowledge expressed in the phrase so loved among the open access community (of which I am a passionate member!), "the sum of human knowledge."

Knowledge, thought of in this way, is one thing added to another, to another, and so on.

This is so incredibly limiting, and a disincentive to learning (as well as being neither useful nor accurate). If your knowledge is everything you know, added together like the items on a list or in a box, then to add one more thing (that is, to "learn") adds very little to what is already a very large number.

But suppose instead that the really important thing about your knowledge is not each item on the list or in the box, but the connections between them. Suppose, that is, it is a network. Not the points on a map but every possible road between them. Now when you add one more point that really large number becomes unimaginably larger in an instant. And every new thing you learn has the potential to grow it unimaginably more; and each new point on the network adds more connections, more potential than the last.

Instead of something arduous with diminishing returns, lifelong learning becomes a dizzying, accelerating adventure bursting through horizons.

And rather than just sitting there, passively, gathering dust, it's almost as though every idea you have, every thought, every memory, every fact, every image, sound, feeling is alive, reaching out into the world looking for things to connect to. Knowledge goes from something dusty and static to something vibrant, active, transformative. Something with the power to bend the world out of shape.

This excitable, enthusiastic, always hungry and constantly rewarding feedback loop is, in essence, what we commonly call "curiosity." And it is the most powerful engine for creativity and change that we have.

Everything in Its Right Place?

Ideas formed from new connections may be the essence of creativity. But what does that really mean?

To understand what makes a new idea creative, think of that traditional saying, "no one stands in the same river twice."

It's true because even if I go and stand today in the same spot in the same river as I did yesterday, I am actually doing something I have never done before. That's because both the river (yesterday's water is now closer to or in the sea) and I (who have a whole set of new experiences) are not the same as we were yesterday.

There is, of course, great wisdom in this saying, on many levels. Most of all for me, it captures the healing power of time, making things possible after time that would have been unthinkable in moments of intense grief or anger. Entrepreneurs might also recognise in it the concept of an idea that is before its time.

But it also captures something else important. Not all differences are the same, as it were. Some are truly innovative. Some are ridiculous but utterly useless. And some are different in name only. The first two of these are where creativity lives (because you never know which ridiculous things are just ridiculous, and which are revolutionary until you explore). The other is, for our purposes, dull and to be avoided, but far the most common, because of the lack of variety in our knowledge.

Here is another example to show what I mean. I eat porridge for breakfast most mornings, and just like the person in the stream, the same me never eats the same porridge. So every time I eat porridge for breakfast I am doing something fundamentally different.

But eating porridge at 8 am on Tuesday after eating porridge at 8am on Monday is not something different in a creatively interesting way.

And that's because at the level of ideas, or concepts, eating porridge in the morning is still eating porridge in the morning, whatever morning it is. This sounds obvious. It's actually one of the hardest concepts in the whole of philosophy and I'm not going to get into the full reasons why (if you want to explore in your head, ask yourself how many details you would need to add to the porridge eating scenario for the situations to become really significantly different: an acquired allergy? moving from Siberia to the Sahara? being underwater? On the moon? Having run out of porridge and money but knowing there was some on your neighbour's sideboard?).

We only need look at technology to understand that what might feel like a complete overhaul (an agency comes in and "radically redesigns your UX") is actually utterly insubstantial. While a seemingly tiny tweak (changing your blog's font from a serif to a sans serif and as a result opening it up to a whole new dyslexic readership) can be revolutionary.

It is this latter kind of connection are we trying to train ourselves to form.

The key lies in one of the commonest aphorisms:

"Everything in its place."

"Everything in its place" is the porridge for breakfast of the ideas world. It describes perfectly how the world ticks over in the same old way with the same old systems operating and the same old effects following on from the same old causes.

And when the problems to which we desperately need solutions (whether that's climate change or how to survive family Christmas without a fight over who carves the turkey) arise from that "same old way," the solutions we seek can only come from shifting something out of its "right place."

The connections creative thinking helps us form are precisely those, ones that shift things out of their "proper place." It might be seeing something familiar in a new light or an unfamiliar setting. It might be combining two things to make something entirely new. It might be taking an idea from one field of expertise and applying it, or moulding it, to another, But what makes something creative is that an element of our familiar world has been rendered unfamiliar. And it is that sense of something being out of place that makes the results of creativity potentially useful.

One of the reasons creativity is so hard is the strength with which we are accustomed to things having a "proper place." Years of experience and centuries of convention have associated certain things with certain other things, certain actions with certain feelings, have made certain ideas fit in certain schemes and made us think to ourselves, "you can't possibly say that" if we so much as imagine them elsewhere.

We often experience this strength of association when we start to let our minds wander only to find ourselves pulling back from certain avenues of thought because "we can't go there" or laughing at the very idea of something so ridiculous as the hybrids and chimaeras our imaginations are on the verge of conjuring. The ridicule of parents and teachers, friends and media telling us "don't be so silly" has become internalised and now we wouldn't dream of such daftness as imagining something out of its proper place—and even if sometimes we wish we could, we find we have internalised those conventions so intensely that we can't.

Exercise 3: "Just So" Stories

Think of something that "must be in its place."

It might be a piece of knowledge that comes from one field that couldn't possibly be transferred to another, or something that just has to be done a particular way: something you'd be embarrassed about suggesting otherwise.

Ideally, this will be something that is so entrenched in your mind as having to be a certain way that it feels strange, slightly uncomfortable even, to make it the subject of an exercise like this. Something you wouldn't want your friends to see for fear of judgement. It could be a moral principle, like "murder is bad"; or it could be a social convention, like "it's good for families to eat dinner together"; or a way of doing things, like eating soup with a spoon rather than tearing the head off a rubber duck and pouring the soup into your mouth through the bill.

Once you have identified this thing that must be "just so", ask yourself why. And keep doing that to see how many reasons you can find. Try to identify where an answer boils down to "because reasons" or "that's the way it's done." And when you do, keep asking "what reasons?" and "why is it done that way?"

And once you have established what the answers about doing things this way are, ask whether you think they provide good reasons. Now you have got this far, you can allow yourself to define "good reasons" any way you want. Indeed, thinking about what you understand to be good or bad reasons for something is a key part of understanding how you see the world. And that in turn is a key part of understanding how you might begin to change the world from how it is to be more like the world as you want it to be.

Finally, think about how the world might be different if that principle or convention or action weren't the default. What might be in its place? What reasons might drive these replacements? What might these alternative worlds look like? What would be the consequences for everyday people if the world changed overnight and they found themselves in this new and unfamiliar one. Would they adapt? How? Would this be a better world (as you define it)?

A final note before we begin.

It's important to point out that shifting things out of place doesn't mean learning in an unstructured way, or being unable to organise things by category. After all, the concept of a "right place" refers primarily to the way simple things have combined into complex conventions (from "Uncle Bill always carves the turkey" to "we need to fly to the conference in Perth").

But it is important to use categories that work for you, that reflect your understanding and emphasise the provisional nature of knowledge. So how this book teaches the art of learning will focus on the relationships between things and the properties of things more than on the names traditionally used for them and the rules traditionally ascribed to them.

To use the classic example from creative thinking, if we think about everything we know in regard to stationery, we might include paperclips when we're drawing up that list. But we won't get so fixed on a paperclip being an item of stationery that we lose sight of the fact it is mainly a mechanism for fastening things together and could come in very handy for clipping things that aren't paper. And we won't get so fixed on it being a fastening device that we lose sight of the fact it is, essentially, simply a piece of wire and can as such come in very handy for things unrelated to fastening.

Learn About Lots of Things

Building your Knowledge Map

In 2010 the BBC aired a landmark series of radio programmes in collaboration with the British Museum. A History of the World in 100 Objects was an attempt to paint as complete a picture as was possible of, well, the history of the world, by focusing over the course of 100 episodes on, again as the title suggests, 100 objects, ranging from a 2 million year old stone chipping tool to a solar-powered lamp (there were actually 103 episodes).

When I was working out the detail of the creative thinking game Mycelium (which I will outline in full later in this book), I decided to see if I could go even further. Could I encapsulate the whole of human knowledge under 100 headings.

These seem like remarkably hubristic exercises. And each (not that I am claiming parity with the BCC or the British Museum when it comes to curation) is riddled with imperfections.

But they represent attempts to undertake an incredibly important endeavour, and one I want to suggest you should also carry out. That endeavour is to map out, in some representative form at least, the totality of your knowledge.

As we've already seen, the key to creativity is building and then using a wide base of knowledge. And, indeed, building it so that you are best able to use it. Fitting that recipe, most of the techniques in this book are aimed at helping you to learn, store, and use as much knowledge as possible in the most fluid and creative way possible.

Building a map of your knowledge as it stands right now is a crucial step in that endeavour. Let me explain why. And then let me explain how. But let me start by explaining what I mean by a knowledge map.

A knowledge map is simply some kind of representative record of the structure of what you know. It can take one of a number of forms, but the key is that it should contain all the important elements that will allow you to use it effectively. I would recommend you don't, at this stage, devote more time than is needed to satisfy these basic elements. We will return to this and similar subjects throughout this book, and each time we do will provide you an opportunity to refine, expand, and adjust your knowledge map.

First, another theme to which we will return regularly. There are different media available to you for creating your knowledge map, as there are for many other of the tools you will use in your creative journey. Some media are more suited to some elements of those tools, and some to others.

One choice, for example, is between writing and drawing. As well as being the most familiar medium for many of us, writing has the advantage of allowing you to articulate ideas very precisely, especially where they convey complex theories you want to convey clearly so that you can return to them with confidence. Drawing on the other hand enables you to relate pieces of information incredibly clearly to each other, and is flexible, allowing you to create connections between ideas or facts; and it involves greater sensory input, which can help make information more memorable.

Another choice is between an analogue system and a digital one. Analogue systems involving the physical process of writing/drawing can be more deliberate and mindful in their construction, and more personal in their form, allowing a deeper connection with knowledge. Digital systems enable you to store vast amounts of information and the flexibility afforded by tagging and metadata allows you to explore all kinds of possibilities you might otherwise miss or find too burdensome.

But most important is selecting a medium that will work for you. The key technical properties your knowledge map must have if it is to function effectively are (again, we will return to these in greater detail when we discuss how to manage portfolios of projects later in the book):

- Usability. Primarily you should be able to understand it clearly, and it should be portable enough that you can take it around with you.
- Flexibility. This is a working tool. It will change. And one of its purposes is to let you play around.
- Simplicity. Specifically, you should be able to see, or at least get to, everything at a single glance. Endless pages of text or immensely intricate diagrams, or spreadsheets you have to scroll miles across the screen to get to the end of can (probably) have a place in your armoury. But this is not that place.

To get back to the matter in hand, here are the uses a knowledge map serves. And for each of those uses we will look briefly at the elements this means they should contain.

- A benchmark.

Knowing where you are right now will help you to see how far you have come as you look back on your journey. In particular, you should be able to see how much you have progressed in relation to the other items on this list. Ideally, your knowledge map will provide you with the visual cues necessary to monitor this without having to go through it with a toothcomb. We will think of those visual cues as we go through this list.

- A schema to capture your beliefs about how the world works.

This could sound off-putting or overly complicated. "Schema" and "mental map" are terms that may seem deliberately obtuse. Unless you have hung around certain quarters of YouTube. In which case they might sound like deliberate buzzwords. They are neither. It's simply the most accurate way to describe a very particular kind of representation of information. In this context, a schema is a representation of how you believe things fit together.

Let me explain. Most of us have a few fundamental belief systems that shape how we think about the world. These will tend to be beliefs about why the world is the way it is, and how we think the world should be. They will be lenses for understanding the past and present, and for considering the future. We use them to understand new things we encounter, to make sense of relationships, to predict what will happen in the years to come, and to weigh up the risks and consequences of actions to help us decide what actions we should, and shouldn't take.

To say that a knowledge map should act as a schema is simply to say that wherever we have fundamental beliefs, frameworks, or desires that influence how we think about the world, the knowledge map should capture what those beliefs are and which things they affect.

Obvious examples would be religious beliefs, such as the belief that the natural world was created by a powerful being. This will affect how someone thinks about all kinds of fields of knowledge from meteorology and natural disasters to insect life and the fossil record.

Other examples are beliefs about human nature, such as the belief that human beings are fundamental good, or fundamentally selfish (what "good" means to you is another such belief). What kind of outcomes people should strive for, how they should be rewarded or protected, the relation of animals to inanimate objects, or people to the rest of the world (are human beings unique, or simply one of many similar creatures). All of these areas of belief will affect how you understand everything from human rights to the nation state to property to how people spend their leisure time.

The Monk, The Mushroom, and the MRI

The reason to capture this information about the beliefs that frame your view of the world is that making them explicit will help you to place new information. It will give you insight into why some things matter to you (such as the reason you feel a sense of burning injustice about deforestation or that people who engage in popular sports are wasting their lives). It will help you to understand other people (by understanding that differences of opinion often come down to something really fundamental about the way we see the world), giving you greater empathy and better conversations. And it will help you to understand what it might take to change your mental frames, the way a scientist who understands the paradigm they are relying on will be able to examine and engage with anomalies.

A way I find helpful to illustrate the different beliefs that create my mental framework is drawing coloured lines around groupings of information like little puffy clouds. This grouping in itself is a cue. And I fill in the details around the borderline.

- A way of demonstrating how different things fit together: in relation to each other; and in relation to wider categories.

No piece of knowledge, or field of knowledge, exists in isolation. The way groups of ideas cluster might be driven by something personal to you, or by accepted norms, but understanding the connections that hold groups of information together is like getting to know the terrain of each country on a globe.

Suppose you know a fair amount about planes, drones, boats, elephants, and seaweed. Your knowledge map would naturally cluster the first three of those together under a common heading of "mechanised transport." That's a vertical relation (a relation between a more specific, detailed subject and a more general one). But there might be other relations that are horizontal. Boats and seaweed, for example, have a common marine setting. Elephants, seaweed, and drones can all be found in large concentrations (herds, forests, and

45

swarms respectively) and so there are things those three might have in common.

Your knowledge map should certainly cluster things together under general headings as a way of simplifying the map. You can represent this vertical grouping in different visual ways, either as a group embracing different points or as a structure that moves literally down the page as it branches out.

You might also want to draw lines between areas that are not part of the same general group but nonetheless have a relation to each other. Or you could put them physically closer on the map the more closely related they are.

- A way of identifying gaps.

It's easy to say "you don't know what you don't know." But you will find there are considerably fewer of these "unknown unknowns" if you undertake an exercise like this one.

Identifying what's missing from the overall landscape of your knowledge will give you an automatic starting place for your next reading, and will enable you to be on the lookout for ways to fill in those gaps. Remember that every gap is not just a single thing you're missing out on but a plethora of possible connections to every single thing you know.

You will no doubt be aware of some of the holes in your knowledge. But the best way to make sure you have found as many as possible is to compare your finished knowledge map with something like the 100 category list I prepared when making Mycelium (you will find a copy of that table in the section on Mycelium later in this book).

One way of highlighting gaps you have is to include at least the broad categories where you have very little knowledge at present, and then to use colour coding to create a heat map, in a way that makes sense to you, and which you can watch progress over time as the gaps disappear.

- A way of identifying common threads.

Maybe you know about France, desert conditions, polar exploration, rainforests, seafaring, and Singaporean food. It might not have occurred to you before, but seeing them laid out like that makes it very clear that you are fascinated by travel.

At a more abstracted level, suppose you identify that you have strong concentrations of knowledge around studying the expansion and collapse of ancient civilizations, reef ecosystems, politics, and strategy games. Seeing all of those together points to an interest, or at least a competence, in understanding competition for resources, and the principles that govern such competition, which is an area in which there will always be a need for creative thinking!

- The ability to accommodate new things and easily adjust in the light of those new things.

This is the most practically important aspect of your knowledge map. It is the element that enables you to learn new things at a faster rate and deeper level by helping you to situate them in the context of what you already know. That way, you avoid feeling as though you're starting over each time you learn a new subject, because your knowledge map provides you with pegs to hang new subjects on.

We will look at exactly how your knowledge map works in this way later on, but some simple examples will show how learning can be accelerated. Suppose you are learning about the development of political and social systems in India. If you already know about the history of China, or France, say, then you will already have some idea that societies and social systems pass through various stages. You might also understand that there are links between politics and local geography or climate or the scarcity and abundance of different resources. That will enable you to start understanding new material more deeply and quickly than if you had to learn about every country without understanding that there might be general principles.

It's this development of a general understanding of the common principles that apply to common systems that helps explain why some people seem to be able, for example, to go from newcomer to expert almost overnight at different board games, and why some people are able to pick up new languages seemingly effortlessly.

General principles such as these need, of course, to be able to shift as new information comes in as well as helping situate that information. To go back to our example, understanding the development of one country might reveal that progress and the presence of natural resources are intimately linked. But your understanding of how they are linked will grow more nuanced over time. Your basic grasp of the concept will show you something vital to look out for as you learn about somewhere new. And it's an incredibly valuable exercise to form the best general theory you can as you go. But new areas and their unique contexts will allow that general theory to develop.

Exercise 4: An Archive of Your Own

Before you construct your knowledge map, or other systems in the book, there is a question you need to answer.

What method of storing information works best for you?

I have arrived at the ways of doing things that work for me largely by trial and error. The more times I've been through this process, the more I've been able to distil principles from it. Such as needing physical rather than digital systems where possible. Such as the importance of colour, line, visual movement. Such as the importance of simplicity and portability. In order to work out which systems, materials, or apps work best for you, it's helpful to think through some of the following questions.

- Are you more at home in the digital or analogue world? Do you write notes to an electronic device or in a book? Do you read books or on a device?

The Monk, The Mushroom, and the MRI

- Do you like to have everything in one place? Or is it more important for you to have the best tools for each specific job you do?

- Do you like to "write things up"? That is, do you make notes on the hoof and then file them in a master system later, or would you rather that once you have written something, the job is done?

Broad Learning or Deep Learning?

The first element of creativity is this: learning lots of things about lots of things. It sounds both daunting (that's a LOT of things!), and simple ("learn stuff": haven't we been doing that since we emerged from the womb?).

It's not really either of those things. It's not as simple as "carry on doing what you've always done" (though it might be as simple as "do what you did when you were a child," as we hinted earlier). Because most of us don't actively learn very many new things, despite the staggering claims we hear about the amount of information passing across the windscreen of our attention equalling this or that numbers of mediaeval libraries or ploughman's lifetimes (the "mediaeval ploughman's lifetime" seems to be the default unit of information in common parlance in much the same way as the Olympic swimming pool has become the default unit of volume and the football pitch the measure of area). Neither am I suggesting you actually lock yourself in a library (mediaeval or otherwise) and surround yourselves with a thousand open books until you have them learned by rote.

Rather, what we will do here is what most efficient problem solvers do. We will break the task down into its parts, grasp each of them, and then see how those parts fit back together to form a whole.

As it happens "learn lots of things about lots of things" has two parts.

They correspond to what might sound like a more familiar distinction. That between broad knowledge and deep knowledge. Broad knowledge reflects a grasp of many different subjects. Deep knowledge reflects that the grasp one has of one or more subjects is firm, detailed, tending to what we might call an expertise.

It's a distinction we find in two numbers that seem to appear everywhere in the work of self-improvement influencers (rather like "pi" or "the golden section" seem to appear everywhere in nature). 20 hours is the figure Josh Kaufman identifies as being the time it takes, if you direct your efforts efficiently, to get really quite good at any subject. On the other hand 10,000 hours, as Malcolm Gladwell expounds in Outliers, is the time it apparently takes to achieve mastery in a subject. Those figures, of course, fail to stand up to scrutiny. But they are useful nonetheless. They hint at two different approaches to learning: the paths of the competent generalist and the expert specialist.

You will, of course, have realised at this point that I will advocate an element of both. These are the two parts of "learn lots of things about lots of things." The way I will express that element of "bothness" is by saying it matters which things you learn, and it matters how you learn them.

Taken together, this mix of broad and deep learning is how you stockpile the raw materials of creativity. Without those raw materials you can't make new things. Because new things are simply so-far untried combinations of existing things (yes, it's not quite that simple. We will come back to "a-ha moments" later. For now, it is 99 and so many nines after the decimal point percent that simple as to be worth proceeding).

But it's not just a case of stashing those materials away. Like a grab bag, or supplies of food, they need to be ready to deploy for idea generation or problem solving at a moment's notice. Both are really good metaphors for learning. Both convey the importance of the contents themselves and the way those contents are stored. One without the other will lead to frustration. Get both together and you're ready for any eventuality. What we will learn now are the techniques to store them in just this way. First, we will look at what to study, and then how to study it.

There is only so much we can learn in a single lifetime. Otherwise we would just learn everything about everything. On the other hand, AI search and Wikipedia between them do a pretty good job between them of knowing enough that if they could talk among themselves they would probably use your super-learning as their equivalent of the "mediaeval ploughman's lifetime." So why learn anything when we could just ask?

As is so often the case, Simon Sinek's very simple maxim applies. "Start with why." Why are you learning?

And that takes us to the next exercise.

Exercise 5: What problem do you want to solve?

Remember the first exercise? It asked what creativity means to you. And I said that your answer to that question would provide much of your motivation for reading this book.

At that stage, we thought very much in terms of the skills you wanted to gain, of the changes in the way you thought, acted, and related that being creative would help bring about.

But those are general things. And you quite probably want all of those things, if you think long and hard enough, for a reason that's particular. Creativity will give you a better chance of solving any problem that comes your way. Maybe that in itself is reason enough for you to be on this journey. You want to be a martial artist of the mind.

Most people's journey, though, begins with a particular problem. Often accompanied by a sigh of frustration, a string of disturbed sleep, and a nagging feeling that you should be able to do something about it but can't figure out what.

And, and this is the bit that matters here, when you start to "learn lots of things" you will take the first instinctive step by learning about subjects related to that particular problem.

So this exercise has two parts. As always, take as long as you want or need to answer each part. And be honest about your answer. That might mean digging around inside yourself. It might mean coming back to your answers repeatedly over the hours, days, and weeks that follow. That's all good. Doing so will help you finesse your answer until it's just right. And that in turn will enable you to use it most effectively as a base camp for your creative journey.

    a. What problem do you want to solve?
    b. What subjects most relate to that problem?

Commentary and prompts

Questions like this, or especially questions like the first one, will almost always lead to that common condition: blank page syndrome. Otherwise known as tip of the tongue/point of the pen idea evaporation.

There are various reasons for that. The first is that the answers tend to feel too large or too small. Huge ambitions to solve huge problems leave most people feeling embarrassed, ashamed, or just silly. There are eight billion people in the world, the reasoning goes. Millions of them are smarter than I am. Everyone knows the climate crisis/clean water/girls' lack of access to education is a problem we have to solve. They're so big the United Nations has devoted goals to them. So who am I to think I might be able to solve it?

On the other hand, personal ambitions to solve personal problems leave most people feeling embarrassed, ashamed, or just silly. There are eight billion people in the world. Millions of them have problems worse than mine. Solving the misery of my family Christmas won't do anything to help them. My life gets better while theirs stays as bad as it is now. So who am I to deserve that?

Embarrassment, shame, fear of being silly. These are direct barriers to creativity. How many problems in history have gone unsolved because people didn't put their hand up and ask "I wonder if this might help?"

Of course it is not your fault if you have this fear. It is the fault of a society that shuns the unconventional, dampens enthusiasm, values peace and quiet and not rocking the boat over the chaos that curiosity can cause. It is the same society whose tendency to act in this way has led to a lot of its problems in the first place.

By the end of this book I hope you will be comfortable writing things that make you squirm now. And maybe proud to share those things as a start to collaborating with others to make them happen. (And on the question of small personal goals, there are many reasons you should seek to solve them, from the fact it's good training to the self-confidence and freed up head space it will give you meaning you can focus on other problems to the fact that your being miserable won't actually solve any of the world's other problems.)

But another reason why answers to questions like this can evaporate on us, even if they seemed really clear in our heads, is that they can tend to be less precise than we think they are.

"I want to clean the oceans" or "I want to ensure everyone has access to a high quality education" are fabulous aims. And they do require highly creative solutions. But they are also very complex. Even imagining what a solution might look like can feel impossible.

The key to removing the imprecision is to allow yourself to say something you know is vague to the point of being useless. And then to start to break down what it actually looks like. Or what a part of it might look like.

I talk about this process of questioning a lot in my previous book, *Living in Longhand*. I will skim over the ideas again now.

Take "I want clean oceans." What does "clean" mean? Is it a maximum threshold for certain chemicals (a reduction in acidity, for example)? Is it clearness, allowing the sun to reach a certain depth? Is it the absence of polluting objects? Which ones? And which oceans do you mean? Are they all unclean in the same way? Are there local factors influencing some but not others? Keep asking filtering questions like this until you arrive at a particular problem, one where you feel you know what a world in which it is solved would look like (however complex and hard the climate targets of 1.5/2 degrees are, they are specific enough that we know what it looks like to work to achieve them).

When it comes to personal problems, we can be even less specific. This often results from a lack of honesty with oneself. And that is fuelled most of the time by the same fear of embarrassment, shame, or silliness I have already mentioned. But honesty and overcoming any shame or embarrassment associated with it are essential if you are going to achieve what you really want. Again, I talk about this a lot in *Living in Longhand*. But let me illustrate.

You might want a "better work/life balance." You might want to travel to nice places that you never seem to be able to visit. Or you might wish your weekends were more fun.

But again, these are vague statements. And the reason this time for the vagueness is that you may not feel comfortable articulating what they mean in practice. Indeed, you may never have articulated that to yourself before. But now you need to (it's also, of course, OK to say "I want to do something fun with my weekends but I don't know what that is right now" and start exploring from there.)

What does the detail look like? What particular activities? What places? With whom? How much would it cost?

You may have an idea which subjects would be a good place to start learning about the problem you have identified. It would also be an interesting exercise to see what an AI chatbot suggests.

And once you have that list of subjects, you are ready to discover what things you should start learning about.

Because they won't be the same.

Don't Learn Things Because You Think They Will Be Useful

If you want to solve problems, shouldn't you start learning things that are useful for those problems? Things that are, in some way, about those problems?

Well...no.

It's always a good creative habit to set your thoughts in motion with something counterintuitive.

The principle I've given in this subtitle, which seems to be, well, wrong, is certainly counterintuitive. But it actually makes good logical sense.

The reason for that is something we have already touched upon, and it's central to creativity. To solve a problem you got into by thinking a certain way, your best bet (the creative option) is to start thinking in a different way.

Think of it in this way.

If there is a really hard problem that you want to work on, then it figures that it hasn't been solved yet (assuming you value the solution rather than just the process in the way you might if you were learning maths). But if it's a really important problem, there will be lots of people already trying to solve it. People who have worked really hard on learning everything there is to know about what they think might be useful for solving it. So if you take exactly the same approach they took, why are you likely to do any better?

To put it really simply:

Creativity is about doing things differently from how they've been done so far.

So why would you do them the same?

It is most likely just to lead you right back to the same problem you're trying to solve—or to the same answers others have already tried and found not to work.

That doesn't mean you shouldn't try to understand the problem you're trying to solve. You could spend years of your life on a wild goose chase that way. Worse still, you may stumble across the answer but not realise you've found it and move on.

I would go so far as to say many problems go unsolved because no one has really understood them properly. This is usually because everyone's been looking at them the wrong way.

So, yes, try to understand any problem you're interested in as best you can. But in doing so, be careful about the assumptions you're consuming along with the facts. Fallacies and biases, conventions and habits, the assumption that correlation is causation: all latch onto straightforward facts and become part of a narrative of inevitability.

Points, lines, and systems: understanding a problem

What does it mean to understand a problem?

I'm not going to dwell for a long time on this, because it would make a substantial book on its own. But it is important to know what it means to understand the problem you are trying to solve enough to know when a solution is worth pursuing, but not so deeply or so much embedded in a tradition that you can't see past the assumptions that have prevented solutions up to this point.

There are two sets of interrelated questions here that feed each other, as you will find so often happens in creativity. The first set of questions asks what the details of the problem are. These questions are essential for finding promising ways into a problem. The second asks why previous solutions have failed. These are incredibly valuable for exposing false assumptions about the problem (most failed solutions have failed because they didn't set out to solve the right problem).

Here are the specific questions I want you to get used to asking.

1. What are the individual pieces in this problem?

2. For each element involved in this problem, what is it in itself? (Wording shamelessly borrowed from Marcus Aurelius courtesy of Hannibal Lecter in Silence of the Lambs)

3. What has brought each of those elements to their place in the problem, and where are they heading? For the elements in a situation this will mean looking at their history and their motivation.

4. What are the relationships of the peoples and objects involved in the problem, both with each other inside the situation and outside of the situation? (this is where it gets big and unwieldy but also really interesting. This is the subject of a whole curriculum

not a whole other book, but start with Thinking in Systems by Donella H Meadows)

5. What solutions have people tried that haven't worked?

6. Which of questions 1-4 explains why these solutions didn't work?

Let's use an example.

Kathy and Sam take their daughter Alesha to Sam's family every Christmas Day before coming home via Kathy's family on Boxing Day. Alesha is an excitable, curious, adventurous 8 year old. But every Christmas she sits in the corner without saying anything and just reads the book Sam's parents have given her. She isn't interested in the games they play or food and won't speak to anyone until she's back home, when she's her normal self again. How, Kathy and Sam wonder, can they make this Christmas work for Alesha?

Let's answer each of our questions in turn to see how this helps us understand the problem more in a way more likely to lead to a solution. These answers are intended to be illustrative of a thinking process. They are far from exhaustive (seriously, I could write a separate book just about this one scenario. If you really want that, maybe I'll run some workshops!)

1. What are the individual pieces in this problem?

Some of the individual pieces are obvious. Kathy, Sam, Alesha, Sam's parents are clearly "players" in this act. But some key pieces are things. The book. The games. Of course, the settings, too: Sam's parents' house; Kathy's parents' house; home. Some pieces are more abstract, but nonetheless important for that: games, meals, "Christmas." The very fact that Christmas is a piece with a part to plays suggests that "not Christmas" or "regular routine" is also an implied piece. Other pieces are even more subtly implied. The mode of transport between venues, for example. Or weather at the time of year.

2. For each element involved in this problem, what is it in itself?

I won't go through each of these, but I'll go through an example to show you the kind of details to look for. If you want a real deep dive on this, I recommend that you skip to the section towards the end of the book called "idea hooks" which explains in detail how to break a thing down into its essential components.

For now, the areas to focus on when asking this question are these:

   i. Properties

This means exactly what it sounds like. The actual attributes of the person or thing, such as age, gender, height. But also properties that relate more abstractly to their identity such as parent, school teacher, stamp collector, expert in the history of moth taxidermy and so on.

It will also include personality, and even neurotype.

   ii. Personal associations

These will be the things each person brings to a particular problem. Which is different from the things that bring a person to a problem. The latter we will look at under question 3. These, however, are the memories Kathy and Sam might have, the experiences each has had of, respectively, family, Christmas, books, and games.

These will influence their motivations but are separate from them. To understand the problem in all its complexity, we need to unpick the complex network of personal associations we bring to it as well as the conscious motivations we bring, so that we can use each to question the other and understand it better, always with the outcome in mind of ultimately understanding why we have so far failed to find a solution in order that next time, or the time after that, we might succeed.

   iii. Cultural associations

Alongside personal associations, related but different, are cultural ones. These might be the media pressure to have a beautiful family Christmas. The fact that everyone everywhere seems to talk about coming together being the "real meaning of Christmas." They may be more subtle. Such as the feeling that being together should mean actively engaging with one another, which would make a social game more appropriate as a pastime than solitary time with a book.

3. What has brought each of those elements to their place in the problem, and where are they heading?

This is about the motivation and the story of each piece, both the story up to this point and the place the story is going.

Do Sam and Kathy want to have a lovely Christmas? Do they want to give their parents a lovely Christmas? Do they want to give Alesha a lovely Christmas? Quite possibly they will want more than one of these, but will have prioritised those preferences. Maybe they simply want as trouble free a time as they can manage so they can get on with their lives.

And, of course, Alesha probably had no choice in how she got where she is. But she will have known it was coming, and as a person she has an inner life as much as her parents and grandparents, so she will have made plans and devised strategies around the visits.

It's also important to consider how the pieces without their own "motivation" got to this place, and where they are headed. The book, for example, came here directly through Sam's parents. But that might not be the full story. Why? Is it so Alesha will be quiet and let Sam's parents raise difficult or even traumatic subjects with Sam and Kathy? Is it much more benign, wanting Alesha just to be happy, or to give her parents some peace? Or is it part of a long term play to try and win custody? How and why the book got where it did may change Sam and Kathy's best course of action dramatically.

4. What are the relationships of the peoples and objects involved in the problem, both with each other inside the situation and outside of the situation?

Many of the answers to this question will drive the answers to question 2. It is the fact that Sam and Kathy are married, and that both have parents still alive that forms a central part of the reason why they feel the need to undertake a visiting itinerary at Christmas. They, or at least one of them, still feels attached enough to the convention of "Christmas is a time for the family" for Christmas to feel like the time to undertake such a trip (or maybe it's simply a function of the holiday allowance of their work, in which case everyone's relationship to Christmas is messed up?). Possibly one or both of them has a complicated relationship to books (quite possibly stemming from a book-heavy childhood) that means they don't themselves give Alesha a book. Very probably it is this relationship of parent-child trauma around books that creates in turn a grandparent-grandchild relationship of wonder to the very same books, as Alesha once a year enters the magical world of her grandparents' library.

5. What solutions have people tried that haven't worked?

Maybe Sam and Kathy have tried giving Alesha a book, but their book (or their choice of book) didn't absorb her. Maybe they have told Alesha's grandparents not to give her a book. Maybe they have tried roast goose as well as turkey; Trivial Pursuit as well as Monopoly. Maybe they tried visiting their parents in a different order.

6. Which of questions 1-4 explains why these solutions didn't work?

4 means the parents have thus far found it emotionally too hard, because their own trauma is unaddressed

Looking at the various solutions in turn, might their own traumatic experience of books mean they don't understand how to find a book someone will love. Or that they don't truly believe reading a book is a valid thing to do.

If Alesha is autistic, have they thought how difficult any change from normal routine might be? And is it social convention that stops them considering having the same food as they would on a regular day, or believing that they must visit their parents rather than invite their parents to them?

Exercise 6: Disentangling Problems

Now it's your turn.

Take the problem you identified in exercise five. And as these five questions.

1. What are the individual pieces in this problem?
2. For each element involved in this problem, what is it in itself?
3. What has brought each of those elements to their place in the problem, and where are they heading?
4. What are the relationships of the peoples and objects involved in the problem, both with each other inside the situation and outside of the situation?
5. What solutions have people tried that haven't worked?
6. Which of questions 1-4 explains why these solutions didn't work?

I don't expect you to do a deep dive at this point. At some point you will need to at least go to where your toes no longer touch the bottom. But not today. Today give yourself half an hour. A few minutes a question. Get used to seeing that understanding a problem is a process with several stages. And that each stage is separate from but connected to each other stage.

Set the Problem Aside and Start Learning

When you have a grasp on the problem, set it aside.

Don't worry. You can come back to it. In fact, you can come back to it a lot, because as you now start learning things, you will find yourself constantly wanting to come back and make notes and refinements and suggestions (especially as your now primed brain thinks of solutions, realises they have been tried before and explores why those past attempts have failed). That's fabulous and you should keep those notes and comments as a working document. And if you're using digital note taking tools to work with, make sure you keep each version so that you can go back and see how your thought process has unfolded over time.

But for the purposes of deciding where to start "learning lots of things," with an eye to solving the problem with which you are now so familiar, set the exercise aside.

Go back to the original wording of this section. "Don't learn things because you think they will be useful." That holds the key to understanding what you're doing.

Note that the title isn't, "Don't learn things that will be useful."

The real point here is in that distinction. "What is useful" and "what you think will be useful" will often turn out to be different things. Especially when it comes to big problems. Because most people have thought those same things were useful. And the problem remains unsolved. So probably they weren't all that useful after all.

So the things to learn are ones that aren't obvious to someone trying to solve the problem you face. But to learn them with the problem in the back of your mind.

Learn about what interests you. But don't "follow your passion"

"Follow your passion" is one of the most common motivational sayings. Recently, it has fallen out of favour. And it's fallen out of favour for a really good reason. It doesn't work. And when I say it doesn't work, I don't mean that in the way you'll hear a lot of writers and artists talking about it. When they say it doesn't work to follow your passion, what they often mean is "if you only pursue your pet projects you will learn from bitter experience that no one will pay you for them" or, "If you turn your hobby into a job you will lose your love for it."

When I say it doesn't work, I don't mean that. I do think it's really important to learn about things you love.

No, what I mean is that saying you should learn about the things you love gets things the wrong way round. Because if I were to put you on the spot and ask you, "OK, you're going to go away and learn about what you love. What is that?" you might find it really hard to tell me. Because we don't start off simply loving things, by some random act of chance or because the wind was blowing from a certain direction one day. Rather, we start to love things as we get to learn about them. Exposure comes first, and with it a little knowledge. And from that beginning comes curiosity, and a little more knowledge, and more exposure, and discovering that this thing you have discovered has many hidden layers, many deep patterns, a long history, richly different sets of skills, complex traditions. And from the unfolding of all these layers the kind of passion that drives further learning emerges.

So if you don't know what to learn, the best approach isn't to ask "what do I love?" but "what haven't I been exposed to yet?"

A Pin in the Page

This is a good moment to introduce a theme I'll come back to throughout this book. It's one of the most overlooked aspects of problem-solving, creativity, and pursuing success in any area where people have in the past found it really hard to get results. And it's one that applies in a surprisingly wide variety of arenas.

If I were to say that two of those arenas are evolution and the stock market, that should be enough of a hint for those of you with a little curiosity and/or a little wide reading (though a deeper dive will show you other fascinating similarities, such as the surprising properties of large networks).

Here is the question you face as someone wanting to learn. How do you decide what to do when there are lots of options to choose from and either you have no reliable way of deciding which is "best" or there isn't really any "best"?

You will probably be familiar with the difficulty this kind of question creates in daily life. Too much choice and too few filters creates "empty page syndrome." How many times have you stood in front of a shelf at the supermarket looking at tens of different flavours of snacks all costing roughly the same, all sounding roughly as delicious as each other, all looking equally appealing in their packaging, and spent longer than you would conceivably consider reasonable when you think about it in any other setting executing the task, "buy snacks"?

This is one of two default settings we tend to fall back on in such situations. Doing nothing.

At other times we solve the particular problem of inactivity in the face of overwhelming choice by creating and applying defaults. We've all heard about the tech billionaires who put on the same T shirts every day to avoid wasting time deciding what to wear. And I always have the same breakfast (muesli with protein powder) to avoid having to make choices before I've had coffee. But when it comes to diversifying our learning, or changing our perspective, this is hopeless. The whole point is to avoid our usual defaults!

Both of these responses, inaction and unquestioning defaults, are unsatisfactory responses to the question, "What do I do next?"

At least, they are in the context of deciding what to learn in order to be more creative. But they highlight a really important problem we face every day. **Making decisions is hard.** It uses mental resources. And those resources are limited. So by and large it's a great plan to embrace anything we can do to reduce the resource cost of decisions, and save those resources for when they really count. That's why both inaction (mindfully avoiding tangents) and defaults (such as knowing the next step in a project, or having your breakfast at the front of the cupboard) are really important. This is a subject to which I devoted a lot of space in the book *Living in Longhand*.

But defaults and inactions won't work here.

It turns out that what makes this decision so hard is also a major hint at a solution. There is no way of knowing in advance what we should learn next in order to give us the best chance of solving the problems that matter to us. Indeed, if there was a reliable way of working it out then someone would have done so.

So what resource saving strategy do we have that's actually likely to be effective?

I want to suggest one of the oldest strategies in the book. Literally in The Book, as I like to remind my students when I teach them about brainstorming techniques. Because in the Bible, when people didn't want to leave decisions to the frailty of human choice, they adopted an incredibly effective technique.

They cast lots.

Chance is one of the most important ingredients in truly creative thinking. Indeed, it's the one essential ingredient in the greatest creativity project ever embarked upon: evolution through natural selection.

So why do so many people often overlook chance as a tool? Or worse still dismiss it? They do so for a very understandable reason. It feels important to us to be in control. And if we leave something to chance, we feel that we are giving up control. But it's important to realise that what we experience as control is often just clinging to the comfort of the familiar.

Sometimes being in control of solving a really hard problem, finding a way out of the rut of the behaviours that created the problem in the first place, involves finding a way to jump start the process out of those well-worn patterns.

In some circumstances, taking control of the future means choosing to give over part of the journey to chance.

Those of you familiar with the practice will note that this is a very *mindful* way of approaching decision making. It involves being fully aware of the situation you are in; recognising those aspects that are outside of your control; and finding a way forward through the elements that are within your control, but without trying to force circumstances into a narrative that doesn't fit them.

This is very much the case when we need to do something different from what we've tried before. But we have a set of options to choose from and no really good reason to choose any one of them over any other ("good" being the operative word, the "reasons" we do have are too often the biases and assumptions we want to overcome).

We know from experience that if we try to formulate a reason to pick one or another of our options, we end up either falling back on defaults established by the assumptions we are trying to break out of; or caught in an endless and irresolvable loop that leads us nowhere but older.

Chance breaks that loop. It allows us to do something rather than nothing. And it provides us not just something but something new. Something that might help us with the particular problem at hand. Something that certainly will provide us more raw materials for creativity than we started with.

One very simple technique for letting chance decide for you what you should start learning is the age-old method of putting a pin in the page and seeing what you get.

Preparing the Page

Casting lots or drawing straws as a way of making a decision isn't an entirely random process. Rather it's a way of simplifying things once you have a set of pretty much equal options in front of you.

In other words, before you let chance decide between several options, you need to establish what those options are.

To use chance most effectively, you have to give it the best possible set of options. Fortunately, when it comes to deciding "what to learn about next", there are lots of great pre-made options for us. Wikipedia, for example, has plenty. Or even its analogue equivalents, the giant multiple volume encyclopedias that became such good friends in my school library. ChatGPT will tell you any number of things. Some of them might be true. And I have already described my adventures with the Stanley Gibbons world stamp catalogue.

Choosing a subject at random with a physical book is really easy. With a set of dice that includes two with 10 sides, one with 20, one with 4, one with 6, and one with 8, you will be able to find your way to a random page of most miscellanies.

If you would rather choose a subject by name than its position in a book, you can use a random number generator online to give you a number from 1-26 (you can't use a 20 and a 6 sided dice unless you never want to learn anything beginning with "a") and convert the numbers to letters (a=1 etc.). Once you have 2 or 3 letters you can use a search engine's autofill (on a browser where you've deleted your cookies, to avoid it thinking it knows what you want based on past preferences) to find you something.

Perhaps the most fun of all is to use 3 ten sided dice to generate a number from 000 to 999 and map it onto the Dewey Decimal system[4]. This is the way many libraries arrange their books on the shelves and you can lose yourself in the system itself for hours on end, before you even get started on learning any one thing it points you to. The Dewey Decimal classification starts at 000 with computer science and goes all the way to extraterrestrial worlds at 999. On the way it takes in such delights as fallacies (165), mesmerism and clairvoyance (134), prohibited works, forgeries, and hoaxes (098), Miscellaneous fossil marine and seashore invertebrates (563), and Specific parts of and physiological systems in plants (575).

When I was devising the game Mycelium (more of which later, where you will also find the table) I created a table of 100 different areas of knowledge, with the aim of taking in as broad a spectrum of topics as I could possibly do under such constraints. Using a 00-99 dice to choose an area to delve into would keep anyone occupied for years.

Exercise 7: Preparing a List to Choose From

I hope that's given you some ideas. There isn't much need for commentary on this exercise. It's a very simple case of, "now over to you." Use one of the methods above. Or a completely different way of employing chance. And find the topic you are going to learn about next. I would suggest you choose 2 or 3 topics and learn them together. I will talk about why later. But on an incredibly practical level, it keeps things interesting if you don't have some variety.

In the next section, I will talk about how to set about learning your new subject(s).

---

[4] https://en.wikipedia.org/wiki/List_of_Dewey_Decimal_classes

Learn Lots About Each Thing

There is a reason pub quizzes are really popular. Admittedly, when I spent every Sunday as a third year undergraduate at my local pub quiz at the Holly Bush in Oxford, the attraction was more the free roast potatoes that were on offer than the quiz itself, but many of us love having brains crammed full of strange and intriguing facts. And you only have to look at the popularity of everything from Trivial Pursuit to Schott's Miscellany, and of course a whole gamut of TV shows (many of which I enjoyed appearing on in my youth), to see that the appeal goes far beyond the local boozer.

Much of that appeal, of course, comes from the fact that as a species we like showing off in front of our friends. It's the same phenomenon that drives gossip, and means many of us would rather see ourselves as the Yoda of our friend group than the Luke or Leia. It's something we'll spend time exploring in the next book, when we think about how to tell a story to an audience that makes them want to share it.

But that kind of knowledge in itself isn't what we are talking about when we say it's important to learn lots of things. People will often talk self-deprecatingly about having a "head full of useless information." And while they usually want to elicit the response, "That's not useless, it's really cool!" I would argue that when it comes to creativity it is possible to have a head full of useless facts.

Impressing your friends, and gaining social capital is, of course, a use. Indeed it's a use that can solve some problems. Such as, "How do I get a higher status in my friends group?" or "How do I make sure I'm on the guest list for the best nights out?" But for most problem solving purposes it is not useful to know facts that you can recall when, and only when, you are asked a trivia question, and which you can only use in order to answer those trivia questions.

Which isn't to say a head full of facts is always creatively useless. As we said earlier, **what makes knowledge useless or useful isn't what you know, it's how you know it.** And if you know them in the right way, a head full of seemingly unconnected facts can be incredibly useful.

Indeed, if you have learned them in the right way, unconnected facts won't be unconnected very long. You will soon be able to start joining them up. They will almost, if you have really got it right, start joining themselves, each restlessly seeking out new partners in thought, nudging you with their suggestions when you least expect it.

The methods in this section can best be thought of in terms of a running metaphor. As someone who discovered ultramarathon running in their mid-40s and has the indefatigable zeal for evangelising the sport you would expect of a late convert, I tend to find running metaphors best describe most things. But fear not. Other sporting and, indeed, non-sporting metaphors are available and will be liberally sprinkled through this book.

Knowing facts in the right way is like wearing the right shoes for the conditions you're running in. If you head onto muddy mountain paths, you will need to put on trail shoes. If you don't, you'll slide around and get nowhere fast. If you do, you will be free not just to explore the well-worn trails through the hills but to turn aside whenever the scenery looks enticing and create your own.

In this section, we'll learn how to dress our knowledge in trail shoes so it can run freely whatever the path it picks or beats out of seemingly impenetrable thickets.

This won't just help you to be more creative. It will help you study for exams; it will make your conversation more fluent, and more interesting; help you understand and empathise with people; and make you better able to pull together the ideas and evidence you need to communicate more effectively in day to day life. This will help with everything from being a more effective advocate for causes you value to negotiating a pay raise.

Learn Like a Detective: Interrogate The Subject

Let's start with some questions.

It makes sense that the best way to learn new things is by asking questions. Questions are the clothes curiosity wears, and curiosity is the most powerful engine known to humankind. From your first childhood, "Why?" to "What's over that hill?" to "What happens if I try this?" curiosity drives every meaningful process from our growth as individuals to the development of our great technologies from fire to the internet. As far back as the Bible, our journey to knowledge and discovery began with a question, "Did God say, 'You shall not eat from any tree in the garden?'"[5]

So learning begins with questions. What I present here is a specific set of questions, designed to get straight to the heart of a subject. They provide a firm anchor for everything that follows. But most of all they act like primers, loosening the subject up so that it's ready to start hooking up with other areas.

In part this is because they dig under the surface of what you might call the headline facts.

But in part this actual process immerses you in a subject in just the right manner. Not only do you discover a lot along the way, you become familiar with key terms, seeing them in use and understanding how to generate meaningful searches around them. You get a real understanding of what makes a subject interesting to those who specialise in it, but also of how it sits in a wider context.

Most of all, you get an understanding of the things that, to personify a subject of study, make it anxious. When you ask questions of a new subject, you are not just playing detective. You are playing therapist, psychiatrist, confessor. You are learning not just to ask questions of it but to empower it to ask questions of you.

[5] Genesis 3.1

And that's how innovation starts.

Let's start with the list of questions. Write it down. Print it out. Carry it in your pocket. Apply it to new things in your daily life. Add questions of your own. Think of it as a detective's notebook, the thing they reach for whenever they're faced by a situation they need to understand.

Or you may like to think of this approach as lifting the bonnet on the world. What had previously just looked like a shiny piece of metal turns out to be just the casing for a far more beautiful intricate piece of machinery underneath, the part that really makes the whole thing work.

10 "Key" Questions to Unlock a Subject

1. What are the main unsolved problems in this area?
2. What is the vocabulary this field uses?
3. What one other field does it intersect with?
4. What one other field does it absolutely not intersect with? Now make a link.
5. Where do I think it fits in the landscape of my world view? Why? What is one preconception I'm going to bring to it as a result of this?
6. What's one thing about my overall knowledge map that I'll change as a result of learning about this subject?
7. Who are the most famous people in the field? What else did they do? Who talks about them and why and are there any fandoms or factions?
8. What are the controversies or arguments? What do they boil down to? What are the presuppositions behind each side?
9. If I had to compile a table of 3 statistics related to the field what would they be?
10. What are the questions no one is asking in this field?

Exercise 8: Interrogating the Subject

Before we look in depth at these questions, let's take a moment to apply them in an exercise.

The "exercise before explanation" approach is in itself something that helps the creative process, and primes the brain for curiosity. I find it often helps to embed learning more fully if you do so "on the hoof." Doing something you are not quite sure of, then deconstructing what you've just done with the "answer booklet" is a great way to get inside the mechanics of a subject and fully understand it. It also engages many of the processes involved in deep practice that make learning swifter and more effective (as outlined in Anders Ericsson and Robert Pool's groundbreaking book, *Peak* and Daniel Coyle's *The Talent Code*).

So take a subject, ideally the one you established in the previous section that you want to learn. And pose these questions to it.

Don't overthink.

And don't spend too long. Devote an hour, half an hour, even a quarter if that's all you have right now, to the whole process. Open a search engine or chatbot of your choice. And type in the questions, just as I've written them here, adding the topic at the grammatically appropriate point.

Write down the results in a way that works best for you. Highlight things that stand out. Colour code things that are of interest, or parallels you find in the different answers. Don't go into it with assumptions about the process. Just go with it, see what works. Highlight the bits that need more investigation, whether that's words that make no sense right now or concepts you don't fully (or even partially!) understand.

When you've finished, go back and look up definitions for the terms and acronyms you didn't know; biographies for the unfamiliar names you encountered; explanations for the concepts that seemed strange. As you do so, keep noting down questions you want an answer to, links and references to follow up, and any similarities to or differences from things you already know. No matter how daft they feel.

If you feel yourself running out of steam, or losing track, feel free to change the colour coding or the way you take notes, or even the medium in which you do so.

As you develop this into a feedback loop of research, questions, answers, and orientation, you will start to develop the systems that work for you.

Creative questions in depth

Now let's go through the questions one by one, to understand what each contributes to the process of learning-for-creativity.

   1. What are the main unsolved problems in this area?

This question really cuts to the chase when it comes to creativity, because this is the one area in any subject where you KNOW that something new is needed. And as an outsider entering the field you may just be the one who can bring a perspective that will finally solve one of these problems (That's how it has often happened through history. Why not for you?!).

By discovering these unsolved problems before you do anything else, you are priming your brain for problem solving. You are basically telling your existing knowledge and expertise what it needs to be on the lookout for. That way it can start organising itself in the background looking out for anything that suggests an answer.

And by discovering these problems before you discover anything else, you stand the best chance of avoiding the presuppositions brought to them by lifelong students. Presuppositions that are often the reason why those on the inside can't see where or how to look for an answer.

   2. What is the vocabulary this field uses?

Most fields have their own ways of talking about things. Technically we would refer to that as its "**nomenclature.**" If you play a sport or have a hobby, you will probably use a whole vocabulary that those "on the outside" can't begin to fathom. As a bridge player, for example, I will talk to random strangers about what version of Blackwood they use, whether they play reverse transfers and negative doubles, share stories of a favourite squeeze, coup, or finesse; and debate the merits of 2nd and 4th leads and reverse attitude signals.

Anyone who isn't a bridge player might recognise some of the words but those words will make no sense as I use them.

A question in the 2023 Creative Thinking World Championship played delightfully with the obscure sets of terms groups of people use to set themselves apart from those who don't share their particular interests. Competitors were presented with a circle marked with dots, and beside each dot was the name assigned to a fielding position in cricket (mid wicket, slip, extra cover, silly mid off etc.). We were given the scenario of imagining an archaeologist of the future. The unfortunate soul was fluent in the English language but knew nothing of cricket. We were asked to imagine what they might make of such a diagram. It's a fascinating, not to mention hilarious, exercise to apply in many circumstances. And might be something to try alongside learning the actual meanings assigned to any words or phrases.

Alongside this nomenclature, or general vocabulary, there will be a "**taxonomy.**" This is a classification system. It's the thing that enables you to describe where something fits in a certain world. In sports, for example, teams are placed in divisions. So when someone talks about a first division or a fifth division team, that gives a huge amount of information to help us understand other facets of the team. Age groups are another form of classification, or political parties, or the arrangement of flowers by species and genus.

These two things, nomenclature and taxonomy, provide a framework for understanding how people think, talk, and feel about most subjects. They help you get "inside" a subject. And getting inside a subject, using language the way the people who study or practise it do, even if you don't understand it fully at first, is the surest shortcut to learning. It's learning by practice rather than learning by theory.

This is the equivalent to "immersive" learning of a language. And because you don't *quite* understand it, you will find yourself with a search tab constantly open, and a series of post-its bookmarking your notes as you flick back and forwards to try and figure out where things fit, both within this field and in relation to others you already know. It is exactly this way of approaching things that helps you prepare to use them creatively.

And to use them practically, because learning by practice is already familiarising you with the notion that ideas are dynamic, active things rather than passive objects of rote learning.

3. What one other field does it intersect with?

Start how you mean to carry on. Making connections between your new field of knowledge and others. Think of an area you think intersects in some way with the one you are learning about. It should be something you are familiar enough with that you know its language with passing fluency already.

The purpose is that as you learn a new subject you look for similarities to and differences from another, familiar, one. For example, suppose you want to learn about coral reefs. You might not know much about the seas and oceans, or watery habitats in general. But maybe you know a little bit about rainforests, at least what you have picked up from an Attenborough documentary or two. Maybe you know that the insect and plant ecosystems of the canopies where the sunlight is rich differ entirely from the fungi and ants that make their home on the dark damp forest floor.

This gives you a "way in" to the new subject. Do any of the things you know about rainforests apply to coral reefs? An obvious place to start might be sunlight. Do the areas at the top of the reef where the sunlight is strongest support different or more dense populations from those further from the surface or hidden beneath the reef? What about life on or under the sand of the ocean floor?

The Monk, The Mushroom, and the MRI

There may be no similarities. Indeed, it's a good habit to be on the watch for confirmation bias when you think you have found things in common between subjects (though for learning the practice of creativity it's better to make the associations first and assess them later than to dismiss notions before they form).

But you may be close to the first step towards even wider connections and deeper questions. How does proximity to sunlight affect the kind of life a place can support? What qualities enable some organisms to thrive away from the light?

It is this kind of question that really knits your knowledge together and helps it to grow.

4. What one other field does it absolutely not intersect with? Now make a link.

It can be incredibly useful to find something you are sure has nothing at all to do with the area you are about to study, and then force yourself to look for connections. This is about sending your mind on forays into new territories. Preventing it from staying on the smooth, well-worn trails.

You might be pretty sure, for example, that rugby football is unconnected to coral reefs. You might start by listing some of the key things you know about rugby and then asking how they might relate to coral reefs as you find out more ("priming" yourself as you read and research). Or you might, for example, watch a documentary about rugby immediately before watching something about coral reefs, making written, typed, drawn, or spoken notes as you go, maybe making clips or taking screenshots of the way a shoal of fish moves through a reef like a maul rolls across a rugby pitch.

This might lead you to consider, for example, how separate entities (players or polyps or fish) come together to form something that behaves as though it were a single organism.

And this might lead you to start to ask more general questions again, about the way larger organisms are related to the smaller parts of which they are made. And again, arriving at questions like this is when you can start to have real insights into complex problems.

5. Where do I think it fits in the landscape of my world view? Why? What is one preconception I'm going to bring to it as a result of this?

The most important part of learning any new subject is to establish where it fits in the overall landscape of your knowledge.

The stuff that fills your head is like a map. Except it's a little bit wibbly wobbly. It's more like a three dimensional model built out of straws that you can bend and stretch and twist and play with as you learn and experiment.

It's our mental representation of the world as we see it at any one moment in time, how we understand the way things fit together. It's really important to note that "at any one moment in time" bit. Because that's what makes it highly malleable. And that malleability is what makes it so useful. Not only does this wibbly wobbly internal landscape grow with us, flexing as we learn and correct ourselves. We can also play with it and use the results to change our plans and actions, emboldening us to try things to see whether they support or refute the new models of reality that result from this experimental play.

Most of all this landscape helps us to situate new things we come across. It's why, if we see something we don't recognise in the food aisle at the store, we are likely to think it's edible. Our mental representation of the world tells us that food aisles are for, well, food.

Similarly, if we pick up a book without a cover and start reading, one of the first things we might do is try to figure out from the first page what genre of book it is. That context will help us make the most sense of what we read. If there are lots of words that seem made up, rather than thinking "this is clearly gobbledegook" we might say, "OK, this seems like science fiction, I wonder what these things are," for example.

Let's consider one of the most famous examples of such a mental representation in action-it'll help us to understand this question. Indeed, it will serve as an example to help explain several of the questions I am encouraging you to ask.

In the 18th century, the philosopher William Paley outlined one of the most notable, and notorious arguments, for the existence of God. It is based upon the mental representations we have of the world. But, crucially, which is where the next question is so important, it fails because it assumes those representations are fixed and accurate and shouldn't, even can't, be changed.

Paley describes someone out for a walk on a heath. Suppose, he writes, our rambler comes across a watch in the heathland grasses. They pick it up and examine it. They imagine that anything they come across might be a part of the heathland environment in which they found it. But they very quickly realise it's unlike everything else in the surrounding scene.

It doesn't belong there, as Paley reminds us pointedly.

He credits our observant hiker with sufficient gumption to decide that the watch wasn't a part of the heath. Things start to come apart a little at that point. The hiker rightly concludes that instead of growing like the grass they found it nestling in, the watch was designed and then made by a watchmaker.

Paley goes on to make one of the most famous analogies in Western thought. Some of the things we see around us every day, things like the human eye, are so complex, so perfect in the way their parts work together, that just like the watch we can't possibly imagine that they just grew that way by chance. Their complexity means they simply don't fit in the surroundings in which we find them, just as the watch didn't fit on the heathland. Instead, like the watch, Paley asserts we must conclude they were made from a design. Just as the watch has a watchmaker, so the eye must have an eye maker, and for Paley that eye maker had to be God.

Paley had done some really fascinating and creative thinking because he had asked himself the question I am urging you to ask, "where does this new thing fit in my knowledge map?"

But he didn't ask the second part of the question. He didn't consider whether his knowledge map might drive him towards particular preconceptions. Such as the preconception that "natural" and "made" are opposites, rather than a spectrum with some interesting aspects such as the length of time the making takes. Nor the preconception that complexity implies conscious design. Nor the preconception that the things that *look* complex really *are* more complex than things that look simple.

Nor did he ask the next of our questions.

> 6. What's one thing about my overall knowledge map that I'll change as a result of learning about this subject?

Paley's problem is that he assumed that his representation of the world must be "right". So when he found something that seemed out of place within it, he sought an explanation for it that would also fit with his view of the world.

But it makes no sense to imagine that our representation of the world is "right." In scientific parlance, it is always provisional. It's the best we've got in the light of the evidence we have acquired to date. But new experiences bring new evidence. And just as our mental landscape is valuable in helping us understand new things, so those new things often form evidence that helps us improve the landscape.

This is what I mean when I say our knowledge maps are a bit wibbly wobbly and need to be stretchable and twistable!

To take a banal example, if I see a lemon zester in the food aisle, it might at first surprise me. But I'm not going to say, "Oh, it's in the food aisle, it must be edible." Instead, I come to realise that the food aisle also has items that help me to prepare food, even though they themselves are not food!

This is what Paley failed to do. He failed to imagine that there might be another explanation for the existence of things like the human eye, one that might require him to adjust his representation of the world.

A century after Charles Darwin and Alfred Russell Wallace provided just such an explanation, that of evolution through natural selection, Thomas Kuhn constructed a whole theory around this approach to re-evaluating our mental landscapes. His book *The Structure of Scientific Revolutions* explains how paradigms, the ways people understand the world, shift in response to evidence that doesn't fit, that isn't "in its proper place." I will talk a lot more about paradigm shifts in the next book in this series, which focuses on the communication of creative ideas.

Constantly checking in and asking, "Might I be wrong?" is fundamental to curiosity and creativity. It is where most truly helpful ideas begin.

> 7. Who are the most famous people in the field? What else did they do? Who talks about them and why and are there any fandoms or factions?

The human instinct to take sides doesn't limit itself to sport. When I taught philosophy to teenagers, I would start by teaching some of the great rivalries. Descartes vs Hume;

Plato vs Aristotle, Kant vs Mill. The people first, because we could give them personalities, voices, exaggerate their characteristics, imagine one of them on either shoulder whispering, shouting, or doing dialectic at us as we read. But the ideas were always there with them, as surely as a great player is always mentioned in the same breath as the team with which they had their greatest success. Empiricism and Rationalism; Materialism and Dualism; Deontology and Consequentialism. Those are the great teams for which these most valuable players of the mind strove and thrilled.

This served as a framework for everything that followed. Every time we turned to something new, students would be on the lookout for signs of a competitive binary in action. Which meant they were programmed to be curious, to connect. And they would take sides, Team Hume or Team Descartes. Team Empiricism or Team Rationalism. Which meant they were engaged, and always looking to critique and evaluate.

As an example, I would introduce Rationalism and Empiricism by saying, "Think of Rationalists as people who believe the human mind is active, making choices, imposing itself on the world, churning like a pool of magma in a volcano waiting to erupt onto the world; and Empiricists as people who believe the mind can only ever be passive, reacting to what it experiences from the world, like fast setting mud waiting for the print of a passing foot."

That simple scheme would then follow them around a whole host of subjects from the philosophy of mind ("why do dualists, who believe the mind is not a physical thing, tend to be Rationalists?") to debates about the idea of "grace" throughout Christian Church history.

"What would...do/say?" Sounds like something from TikTok, but it's an incredibly sound way of understanding a new subject. "What would Descartes have said about whether a computer could pass the Turing Test?" for example will not only teach you about Descartes and the Turing Test (a test designed to tell whether a computer could be considered to have a "mind"), it will show you that the same arguments have been raging for centuries. It will teach you how to translate arguments across time, how to use the past to inform the future and avoid history's errors. And it will teach you that at the heart of philosophy are some fairly fundamental questions about what a human being really is, what the mind really is, whether or not we have free will, and that these questions manifest themselves in many different ways.

Find the factions and fandoms in an area, and you will very quickly get to the fundamentals of what matters to it and why.

8. What are the controversies or arguments? What do they boil down to? What are the presuppositions behind each side?

Of course, binary frameworks are almost always partial glimpses of the truth at best. And I would always introduce my lessons by saying, "this is an oversimplification at best, and at worst altogether wrong," while adding, "but it's really useful."

This question represents the next stage. A way of deepening a framework beyond an oversimplified partisan binary.

What do Descartes and Hume really disagree about? Is it really just about whether the human mind is a part of the natural world or something separate from it? Or is it not that simple? This might lead you to ask critical questions about the personal and cultural situations of the personalities involved. You would discover that while the same currents run through the history of a subject, it's not really the case that we are having exactly the same fights today we have always had. Or that Descartes and Hume are interchangeable with Plato and Aristotle.

In the case of Descartes and Hume, you might start unearthing questions about why philosophers from Scotland and England have been seen as having a different take on things from those in mainland Europe down the years. And those questions might lead you into debates about why there was a revolution in France in the late 18th century but not in the British Isles. And so on.

9. If I had to compile a table of 3 statistics related to the field what would they be?

Figures never give a full picture of anything. But they are very good at giving an instant snapshot of most things.

This question is shorthand for identifying what you believe, on a first pass, are the most important elements in any field. Think of it like the Olympic motto, "Citius, altius, fortius" (Faster, higher, stronger). If you were studying climate change, for example, a key statistic might be 2 degrees, the maximum temperature rise to which the Paris Agreement committed. You might put it even more starkly: "450 parts per million of CO_2 in the atmosphere equates to a 2 degree temperature rise."

It will be really interesting for you to keep a journal of how the things you identify as the most important statistics in a field change as you learn more. What you identify as being important tells you a lot about how you understand the subject.

10. What are the questions no one is asking in this field?

This is a question that will stay with you throughout your time studying anything. It may also lead you into some deep and possibly life-altering areas. If you find the really important questions that no one is working on, you could change the world in truly profound ways.

It's also great for developing the skills that will benefit you in creativity, because the way I propose you do it makes a virtue out of looking ridiculous. And as we've already seen, this is a crucial part of getting the creative ideas to flow!

Let me explain. Many of the greatest breakthroughs in understanding come when someone asks a question that no one else has asked before. Like the first time a geologist looked at a fossil they'd found in the middle of a rocky landscape and said, "This looks really like something that lived in the sea. How did it get here?"

There are almost certainly questions in most fields that the experts aren't asking. And if you can find those questions you could really be on to something. But in a much more banal way, there are also lots of questions it feels like people should be asking as we encounter new material, but they're not, and that's because once we understand the subject a little better we realise there's a very good reason they're not. There might be a rule or a principle that you can rely on in such situations, for example. Or maybe people used to ask many years ago but then someone discovered something that became fundamental to understanding the subject. One that became so fundamental that it could be taken for granted, and used as a starting point.

It's really important that we keep asking those questions as they occur to us, even though we might think it makes us look stupid to do so. And even if they have "obvious" answers. Because doing so effectively replicates the learning process the whole subject has been through as it has formed up to this moment in time.

Type the questions into a search engine or ask someone. It's this kind of childlike "why" that really cements your understanding of a subject, because, and this is the key point: the questions that come into our head as we go through new material are simply the external manifestation of our brain's attempt to sort the material. Pursuing those questions is the surest fire way to hasten that sorting process, and enable your brain to assimilate the expertise of the field in the way that makes most sense to it.

And just occasionally, the unique perspective we bring to this new area means we might stumble across a question no one really has asked before. But if we're not willing to put our hand up and look like a fool we'll never know.

Exercise 9: Further Enquiries

Now try this approach again. Try it with a different subject from the one you picked at the start of this section. But keep that other subject in mind as you do. Be conscious of similarities and differences. Be aware of the ways the vocabulary, the arena of debate, and the "stakes" in that debate differ from or are similar to the first subject. Note those down as you go.

Learning Things to Use Them Not to Store Them: The Power of Projects

One of the most effective ways of learning things such that you can use them creatively at appropriate moments is, as is so often the case, by doing just that: using them. As you go along. And the very best way to help you practise that is by having several projects on the go at any one time.

I devoted considerable space in my previous book, *Living in Longhand*, to the concept of projects and how to pick projects to work on that would fit with, take you nearer to attaining, or actually be a part of the goals you have set for your life.

I won't repeat that section at length, but will explain a very little about what I mean by a project, and how projects help you to learn "about lots of things." Then we will look at how to undertake projects so that they feed your creativity. That undertaking will, of course, start by asking the questions we have just explored.

A Portfolio of Projects

The framework I introduced in *Living in Longhand* thinks about the things we spend our time working towards on different timescales. At the top level there are Sustainable Life Goals. These are the things that, in the broadest sense, express what we want our lives to be like. They might include "creating an impact", "collaborating", "communicating". And they might include attaining and maintaining a certain level of health, financial security, and relationships. Everything else we do in life feeds these Sustainable Life Goals.

The next level down is the "vehicle." These are long term ways of helping you live out those goals. By long term I mean 3-10 years. Long enough to complete your studies, to develop a business or a career, truly master a skill.

At the very most granular level are tasks. The actual things you do every day. The building blocks out of which your goals are, ultimately, crafted. The words you write, letters you send, books you read, workouts you do, food you eat, conversations you have.

And between vehicles and tasks fall "projects." Think of these as "seasons". Quite literally, because they are things that take around 3 months. They feed into vehicles, providing additional context and structure for those larger, longer-term undertakings. And they are made up of particular tasks. They are the equivalent of a paper or a module at college, a sports season or training block.

Learning a new thing is the perfect kind of "project." And, because life is made up of a complex and nuanced web of goals, the richest and most fulfilling life will involve projects of all different kinds in sequence. And several in parallel at any one time. And that means the project is also perfect for creativity's requirement to learn "about lots of things."

Having several projects on the go at any one time also works for my particular neurology and temperament.

ADHD means I am very good at focusing on one thing for hours at a time, but very bad at focusing on one thing for days or weeks at a time. Focus comes naturally to me. I find it relatively easy to go from the inertia of "How do I start this thing?" to the familiar feeling of "How did it get dark already?" But directed focus on a single thing for a protracted series of days is really unnatural. And trying to develop it is the one way guaranteed to up the inertia to unsurpassable levels.

For most of my adult life society has taught the importance of devoting ourselves to a single task in order to gain mastery. Careers, accolades, breakthroughs have belonged to those who have managed those 10,000 dedicated and undiluted hours.

The Monk, The Mushroom, and the MRI

Fortunately for me, several factors have aligned to drive a shift towards the value of the generalist. Some of these are socio-economic, such as the rise of the portfolio career in the face of increasing occupational precarity. Others come from a business or academic environment already rich in specialism after decades of that erection of travel, where added value comes from added perspective.

But there is also a realisation that so many of our most pressing problems are "wicked." That is, they are complicated across so many levels and involve so many moving parts and the intersection of so many systems that specialism can not only never hope to solve them: even trying to solve them by specialism would be a category error.

It is this backdrop that has made creativity so valuable. And ways of learning things that best suit creativity have become superskills. And within that set of superskills, the portfolio of parallel and serial projects–reaching out to, blending and meshing with, informing and iterating each other–has the most exalted place of all.

Your portfolio of projects should cover different subjects, relevant to different areas of your life. That way you're not "specialising by stealth." It also keeps you interested. And whatever your mood level, whatever you feel inclined to do on any particular day, there will always be something to work on.

A Variation on Parallel Projects: Reading Two (or more) Books at Once

Having two or more books on the go at any one time is something that most of us will relate to. It's not just a sign of a magpie mind. Or a way of ensuring there's always something to hand wherever you find yourself. Or about having a book for each mood you might be in.

Setting out not just to have multiple books on the go, but to read them in some way "together" is a great way to get more than you otherwise would out of each. As you read each of them, seeking common threads between them can then help you extract some general principles you can think about applying in many other situations.

Anyone who follows my newsletter will know that I have started writing "multi-book reviews" that focus in on the ways whatever books I have been reading shine a light on each other and the broader world. Probably the best way to illustrate how the process works is to reproduce one of those reviews here and let you see how the threads intertwine.

The two books I have just finished as I write are Anthony Seldon's *May at 10*, an 887 page tome that's one of a series of books by the author about the time in office of British Prime Ministers; and Rana Foroohar's *Don't be Evil: the Case Against Big Tech*. This is a fascinating look at the dangers posed by the huge tech platforms Facebook, Amazon, Apple, Netflix, and Google.

Both are highly entertaining reads. And I found both challenging. The account of May's time in power because I am so far from having a natural affinity for May or her politics– while at the same time, 10 years after I was on the group that drew it up, having taken part in the government review of the Debt and Mental Health Evidence Form that she personally instigated in order to drive fairer results for those with mental health issues. That had felt incongruous at the time and made me suspicious but curious. That same incongruity is writ large in this book.

And I was challenged by Foroohar's book because while I have very much a natural affinity for her economics (which feels as though it sits well with Raworth, Mazzucato, even Piketty) and her ideological case against both the exploitation of information asymmetry against the public; and platforms that become so large they act as innovation-stiflers, I nonetheless have for a decade or more considered myself a part of the ideological nexus that includes the open access movement. And she takes full aim at that movement as being an unwitting (at best) proxy for big tech.

I found, as I always do, both those challenges fruitful. And having to think deeply around them has added nuance to many sharp edges in my ideas.

But what was fascinating was the emergence of two particular themes that run through both.

First is the way transparency, empathy, and bluff can drastically change not only relationships but history.

Second is the realisation that holding power and wielding power are two utterly different things.

Both of these ultimately hinge on the same point. Momentum belongs to those who understand what the levers at their disposal are, and are able to use them. We return, as we so often do, to what I call viscosity–the relationship between our inner world and the external world in which we found ourselves. History favours those whose viscosity is low– because they understand themselves fully; because they understand their context fully; because they can put themselves in parts of that context where they are most efficient; and because they are able to utilise that position effectively.

Narrative is also vital to any wanting to make progress. To understand someone else's position you have to understand the narrative in which they situate both themselves and you, and what their dynamic within that narrative is.

To understand how to control the read someone has on your position, you need to understand fully what your own narrative is, how you and they fit into it and how you wish to move through it. Then you need to understand whether it will benefit your position for the party you are dealing with to read your narrative in this way. If so, then you need to work on providing absolute consistency and clarity–live out authenticity. If not, you need to figure out the narrative that will best support the read you want them to have, and then present that narrative and your respective roles within it in a compelling way.

For any negotiation to succeed, it must be clear to both parties that

- There is a shared narrative;
- Both parties' motivations can be met within that shared narrative;
- There are easy steps each party can take to achieve them without deviating from that narrative.

You also have to understand that making something clear to both parties, in particular that tangible outcomes are achievable, is not the same as making those outcomes achievable.

Whether it's big tech and consumer autonomy; or May's Tory party and its various negotiating partners, it is clear that in neither case were both sides' tangible goals actually achievable. Big tech succeeded in bringing consumers along by "making it clear" that both goals could be met in a framework of data sharing left at companies' discretion. They did that by two means: maintaining an information asymmetry (without exposing it as such through performative transparency), and convincing people that other goals than actual autonomy were actually paramount to them (by misdirection).

May on the other hand failed because she tried to adopt the well-worn negotiating tactic of ambiguity to allow people to read their own goals into a narrative. But ambiguity as a tactic requires ground conditions: trust; maintenance of the credibility of the ambiguous outcomes; the appearance of clarity; and a willing opponent prepared to do without specificity. She had none of these, and her fatal flaw was not realising she had none of them

But there is more than strategy at play in the differing fates of Theresa May and big tech. What comes through again and again in the account of May's premiership is that she doesn't understand how to wield the power of her office. She doesn't understand that driving consensus involves empathy, understanding, building consensus, not just the aggregation of evidence.

Big tech, on the other hand, understand exactly what they are doing. Foroohar uses Brin and Page's early position papers to show they knew exactly how ad revenue would corrupt search integrity, for example. And her insider accounts tell of a strategy across big tech to drive growth and influence regardless of known consequence–consequence that is then obfuscated and, importantly, able to be obfuscated by dealing with a regulatory and legislative regime as well as a consumer base, that sits on the wrong side of an information asymmetry created by the very industry they are regulating: data.

The final takeaway from reading these together. To get what you want in a situation, you must:

- Understand who you are;
- Understand the position you are in;
- Understand the wider context you are in;
- Understand how who you are can use the position you hold most efficiently to get what you want effectively;

- And then build a narrative that brings others willingly on board in making that happen, which requires understanding who they are, what they want, and how they perceive their relation to their situation.

Exercise 10: Reading Together

Pick two books about not obviously connected topics. Read them at the same time. That could be a bit of one in the morning and the other in the evening. It could be alternating days. It could be one book for home and one for when you're out. One for the bus and one for the bath. Whatever works practically. When you have finished, write a review like the one I wrote above, teasing out the common themes of both books, and focusing on conclusions you can take away both into your life and into the rest of your learning.

Effective reading for creativity

How to read could be the subject of a whole book in itself. Reading is something many of us take for granted.

A note before we start. I have spent nearly two decades in the book world. I published my first book back in 2007. From that moment on I have been an "indie" author. I publish my own books without looking for a publisher. The only exception has been contributions to curated volumes, whether that's poetry, short stories, or academic articles.

There are many reasons I took this route, but the one that matters here is that the book world has a lot of very fixed ideas about how things "should be." For a "creative industry" that's not a very creative approach! And it's one I couldn't cope with being boxed in by.

One thing people in the book world have some very fixed ideas about is what "reading" means. There is a lot of snobbery around audiobooks, for example. I am not going to be giving specific advice on the mechanics of learning from audiobooks. But only because that doesn't work for me as a medium. For many it is way more effective and enjoyable than print or screen. But I want to be clear. There is no "real" or "best" way to read. There's just the one that works best for you. (I am also a competitive speed reader. I have won the European Speed Reading Championships 3 times, reading at a speed of around 1000 words a minute. If you think there's snobbery around audiobooks, you should hear what people have to say about speed reading–interestingly, many of them quite happily bemoaning the fact they will never live long enough to make it through their to-be-read pile!)

The principles behind reading for creativity-focused learning are pretty much the same however you read.

I hope it's clear that what I want to outline here is a very specific form of reading. I would hope that you find it enjoyable, because enjoyment is one of the most essential ingredients for the success of any pursuit in life. But while a large amount of reading we do is for nothing other than pleasure, and that is hugely important, this kind of reading is more functional. It is reading that we undertake specifically for a particular goal. The goal of helping us to be creative. I am not suggesting you take a marker pen and a commonplace journal to your sunbed as you sit down with a beach read (though if you want to, you do you!!)

A final point of clarification. Let's assume that what you are reading is non-fiction. For me, these techniques work equally well, and are just as enjoyable, for fiction. But many of you won't be ready to hear that yet!

As we did with the questions to interrogate a new subject, let's break the process of effective reading down into 10 key stages.

1. Don't approach a book cold. Read the back cover and any puff quotes to warm you up. Flick through Wikipedia.

2. Spend a few minutes outlining on a single side what you already know about the subject, in particular noting your assumptions, feelings and any conclusions you may have reached already. Use the questions you learned in the previous section to help you do this. Some of them you may not be able to answer until you have finished the book. Keep these questions either in mind or on a piece of paper you use as a bookmark so you are constantly looking for the answers as you read.

3. Skim the structure of the book and get a sense of its architecture before you start reading. Read as quickly as you can without skipping anything.

4. Any time something catches your attention that you want to remember, or come back to and think about some more: stop, highlight it, and move on.

5. Any time something challenges your assumptions; any time something connects to another subject; any time something resonates with you because it makes a

point beyond the scope of the subject of the book; or where you strongly disagree with the way the author has made their case: stop, highlight, write a brief note in the margin (e.g. "that's like..." or "assumption. Not proven by the evidence cited.")

6. Once you have finished, go back and take notes based on the passages you have highlighted and commented on.

7. Pay particular attention to any comments you have made. Especially where those comments question either your own preconceptions; or the reasoning of the author; or where they relate what the author is saying to a wider context.

8. Make a point to compare and contrast what the author is saying about the subject with what others say.

9. Identify the key themes of the book. And make a note of the author's reasoning and conclusions on each of them.

10. Look for reviews or discussions of the book online or elsewhere. See what others have said about it and whether their conclusions are different from yours. If they are, think about whether you might learn from that–either about the book, or about the kind of people who respond differently to it. This will help you to finesse your own thoughts and response. It will also help you understand the wider landscape of which you are becoming a part, and the kind of problems and concerns it has.

If you find it hard to imagine not keeping your physical books in pristine condition, you might want to start by doing this with ebooks, since it involves interacting with the text! This is especially true for library books, of course!

You can write your notes directly into whatever app or journal you use to keep track of your reading and conclusions from it.

What this process should leave you with is a set of notes that pose questions, raise problems, suggest patterns. These are all things that you can carry with you as you explore further both the direct subject of the book and your wider learning. These themes and questions are connections waiting to be formed, the richest raw material creativity has.

Techniques for Managing Your Project Portfolio

Having several projects on the go at any one time will require finding a way to keep track of them that works for you. It will need to have three ingredients:

1. It should help you organise your thoughts on the project in hand in a way that helps you learn;
2. It should be flexible enough that you don't build walls around any individual project but are able to let it "talk to" everything else you know and are learning;
3. It should enable you to pick up any project and start working on it with the minimum possible amount of activation energy.

Resource Specific Task Lists

I will take the last of those first, because it's the one where I've worked hardest to develop my own system (for the first two, I will share a very brief outline of some tools developed by others, but refer you to their work, which outlines those tools far better than I could).

I go into considerable detail in *Living in Longhand* describing the "resource-specific task list." I Here, I will outline the principle and mechanics more briefly.

For most of us, not all time is equal. We might have little pockets of time in a day when we can pursue a project. But what comes before or after that pocket; what time of day, week, month, year it is; our mood; or state of caffeination; our health; a whole host of factors will mean that some pockets of time afford the opportunity to do deep, strategic, thoughtful work while others might see us lucky if we can remember how to tie a shoe lace.

The key to getting the most out of your time is to dedicate those precious, "golden" pockets of time to the most intellectually demanding tasks (and not waste them on things we could do while half asleep). And to use the near useless ones for doing the tasks that don't require us to be anything more than near useless (don't try to do more than this or you will just sit there in front of a blank screen doing nothing but panic or despair).

We can optimise our time (and avoid wondering "what now?" every time we sit down) by creating, for every project, 3 different levels of task list. Each should contain only tasks that will contribute to the overall goal of the project. Each task on each list should be specific enough that you know what it entails. Each task on each list should fall vaguely into the "what comes next?" category (rather than "something to be done 6 weeks down the line") to keep you heading in the right direction.

But the tasks should be divided up into three lists according to the amount of mental clarity/alertness needed to undertake them. One list should be for things that require your very best time. For me that would be things like "write 300 words of the talk on..." or "compose this week's accessibility newsletter" or "practice memorising cards for 30 minutes". One should be for "meh" time. Which might be "edit 1000 words of my book on..." or "make notes of the last 3 chapters I read." And then there's the more mechanical kind of task I can do without too much thought such as "write the SEO for my blog on..." or "format the slides for my talk on Friday" or "read the next chapter of a book and highlight passages to come back to."

Whatever actual method you use for managing your projects, make sure that for every project these lists are easily accessible. That way, whatever you decide to work on, and whatever quality of time you have to work on it, you will be able to make the most of your time.

Project Management

The best mechanics for how to manage this kind of project portfolio will vary from person to person. I am incredibly analogue, for various reasons most of which come from my ADHD. That means I use a single notebook, a couple of folders and pens and paper for almost everything I do. Most of the gurus you watch on YouTube will talk about their favourite apps. Some of those apps are even the subject of YouTube videos about how they have attracted a cult-like following on YouTube.

You should find a way that works for you. That will mean experimenting and engaging in the one practice I would recommend to almost everyone I speak to: absolute honesty with yourself.

But whatever medium you use, a couple of organising principles can help. And for those I will go back to what for me will always be the *locus classicus* for "information stored ready to use." The stamp catalogue.

The organisational principles that gave me so much information and pleasure, and sparked so many journeys of the imagination, are ones to think about incorporating into any system you use.

The principles below all relate to the way information is presented. Each successive principle grows out of the previous one in an organic way, as you move from the detail of how you take notes on a single subject and progress outwards to the overall structuring of those notes.

- An **intuitive ordering of information**. This is a question that has interested writers and thinkers go back to and far beyond Aristotle. It is still something that taxes anyone who has a collection of information they want to use. What makes sense to you is something that only you will figure out. I am, however, aware that is singularly unhelpful as practical advice. So why not start by arranging information according to the 10 questions we identified in the previous section?

- **Consistency of presentation across subjects.** If you present the information on one subject in the same way, under the same headings, as information on other subjects, that will make it easier to look for, and spot, connections between things. One of the very best examples of this is my favourite game as a child, Top Trumps. Top Trumps cards give the same 5 or 6 pieces of information about multiple different things, not just encouraging but demanding comparison.

- **Easy cross referencing**. If consistency is about being able to compare a second thing to a first thing once you have located that second thing, cross referencing is about making sure that whatever two things you want to compare or think about together, you can do so easily. I'm going to add a note here about the difference between digital and analogue systems. Digital tools make cross referencing really easy. They allow you to tag things and file things in such a way that you can find what you want in a click. But there are downsides to this. It makes it very difficult to stumble across things by accident when compared to flicking through actual physical pages.

These first three principles relate to the internal structure of the system you use. The next three are slightly different, but equally important if your system is to be practical. And that practical usefulness is absolutely fundamental. Too many techniques and tools fail not because their design or their purpose is flawed. But because we don't use them.

Sometimes this is because they are unwieldy. Like the excessive aesthetics of some designer garments, some portfolios are simply impractical. But more often it is because we are afraid. I call this "new notebook syndrome." It's a form of perfectionism. The same perfectionism that we touched on earlier in this section when I mentioned some people feel a horror at writing in or dog-earing books. The same perfectionism that stops you sketching on a new piece of paper in case you make a mistake. The same perfectionism that stops you making a mark on a blank page in case you "spoil" it.

We all know that in theory creative people, like those who succeed in any endeavour, make mistakes freely. They are happy with imperfection. They cross things out, redo them, tear things out, scrunch them up, and rework them with seeming abandon. (Of course, that seeming abandon is often hard won).

I will come back again and again in this book to the importance of letting yourself make mistakes. More important, I will come back to exercises you can do to make it easier to allow yourself to "spoil the page." But something I have found incredibly helpful is knowing when to get myself "the right equipment" and when to get "just anything that will do." It's taken me at least 4 decades to fully learn this and put it into practice.

I use incredibly cheap and ubiquitous exercise books for my most essential journaling and creativity. It "doesn't matter" whether I "spoil" them. So I use them freely. I cross things out. I start over. And as a result I create something useful and, as a result, aesthetically pleasing. If I want a "beautiful piece of kit" as a treat, I treat myself to a folder or a pen, things that I can use again and again without marking or spoiling.

With that said, the second set of principles for your system is:

- **Usable**. This is the single word that captures "all of the above." For a digital system, what it means is that you should use an app/programme that you can use easily on a device you will always have with you. And you should find the interface intuitive and easy to use.

- **Flexible**. Changing the way you think about a subject or, indeed, about the world is a key part of the creative process. As you learn more and more your mind will constantly find itself shifting and shuffling those things. The system you use to manage your projects should be flexible enough to allow it to follow your mind's lead. If you have to abandon the whole thing and start from scratch every time you change your perception, you will find yourself coming up with reasons to stick to the mental structure you already have. And that's the enemy of creativity!

- **Unified**. To make your system easy to use, you need to be able to keep it all in one place. Otherwise you are bound to end up losing bits, or leaving behind the bit you need, and eventually you end up in the same situation as with an inflexible system. It becomes easier to simplify and forget the idea of having multiple projects on the go than it is to keep track of them all. And, again, this makes creativity very hard.

Commonplace Book

The rediscovery and popularity of the commonplace book owes a lot to social media. This is a technique that flourished in the Renaissance, the Enlightenment, and the 19th century. And all of those periods have become the subject of devoted fandoms on social media. The paper-based nature of the commonplace book, and the association with note taking, sketching, scrapbooking, and dusty libraries all also appeal to variations on the highly popular dark academia aesthetic. Which is to say that you will quite possibly see more people pointedly carrying around and photographing themselves with commonplace books than actually using them.

On the other hand, another social media staple actively encourages their use. And that's the flip through. Artists, sketchers, casual observers of life, diarists, and academics have taken to video media in droves simply to flip through the pages of completed notebooks. It's a beautiful phenomenon (though trying too much to emulate many of the examples you will see could cause cases of blank page perfectionism so be careful).

The commonplace book is a very simple concept. It is a single book in which you keep notes, quotes, clips, factoids and ideas you will want to return to.

If you decide to use this method, it is very easy to get lost down one or many stationery rabbit holes as tweed and cashmere toting influencers battle it out over the relative merits of Moleskine, Leuchtturm, Hobonichi, Travelers' Company (nee Midori), Paperblank, Peter Pauper, Clairefontaine and other titans of the journal world. And that's before we get to pens or inks or stickers. All of them are beautiful. Many of them are eye wateringly expensive. But what's actually functional will be personal to you.

You will find lots of advice on how to use a commonplace book, but the key for using it for creativity is to keep in mind the six principles we outlined at the start.

- Ordering of information
- Presentation of information
- Cross referencing
- Usability
- Flexibility
- Unity

Some suggestions to help you with these include, but are not limited to:

- Having an index or table of contents. Or at least, some way of
    - enabling you to see everything at once;
    - that orders or categorises those things in a way that makes sense to you;
    - and lets you navigate straight to any one particular item.
- Using post-its to mark things you want to be able to get to without having to use the index/contents.
    - These can be different colours for different themes;
    - You can also write on the part that sticks out of the book.
- Using markers on the edge of the page. This is a way of navigating to particular topics that doesn't involve things that could fall out or tear off like post-its. If you run a marker pen down the edge of the page then when you hold the closed book you will be able to navigate to individual pages. Some people use different colours for different topics. Others put their lines on different parts of the edge of the page.

- Use stickers on a page so that when you flip through you can see the topic covered (or any other shorthand you want to use) at a glance. This might be slightly less convenient than being able to go straight where you want, but having to flip through to find something (knowing that you will be able to find it) can lead to so many happy little accidents on the way!

- Make key details stand out. Again, something to aid the flip through. Drawings, bold headings, underlining in different colours, writing different kinds of thing in different colours, using highlighter pen. All sorts of things can aid the (re)discovery process.

- Use mind maps. Mind maps are a fabulous way of giving information flexibility by enabling you to use visual cues to connect disparate parts of the page. They also satisfy the unity criterion by keeping things on a single page and are great ways to arrange information logically with the trunk and branch structure. And they are great for helping you both slot new information into your knowledge map, and adjusting your knowledge map as you encounter new information. There's a lot wrong with mind maps, but they are perfect for use in something like a commonplace book for making your notes work for you creatively. For more on how to create and use them, Tony Buzan's *Mind Map Book* is one of the all-time great textbooks.

- Rewriting/writing up. Making notes on the fly and then writing them up in your commonplace book (or other system) carries risks. Specifically, you can lose things in transit, and if you don't write things up regularly the "to be copied up" pile can reach overbearing proportions that just make you feel like giving up. On the other hand, at a practical level, it's easier to carry a small notebook or a waterproof one than a large commonplace book. And rewriting serves a mental function ,both of allowing you to process information, filtering it and assimilating it and priming it; and in terms of helping you learn it by repetition.

Zettelkasten

The zettelkasten method has all the flexibility you could want. But it is less portable than a single book.

Those of us of a certain age will have grown up transfixed by something very mechanically similar to the zettelkasten: the card catalogues that libraries used, where each book had a card, and the cards were arranged in such an order that you could flick through them to find the thing you wanted, and then use the information stored about it on the card to go and locate the full book on a shelf.

We also grew up with rolodexes where we kept people's contact details, and boxes of index cards that we used either to learn subjects at school or keep a record of everything from recipes to record collections.

Zettelkasten means, literally, "box of cards." It is the generic term that applies to each of those methods, and any other method of filing information on cards for cataloguing, storage, retrieval, rearrangement, and use.

Like the commonplace book, the zettelkasten method of arranging information has garnered a considerable following thanks to social media. But where the commonplace book's popularity has become a staple of a certain kind of aesthetic with an intellectual twist, the zettelkasten owes its popularity to the self-improvement and productivity movements.

Its appeal lies in part in the ease with which it can be given a digital life. Tagging information and allowing people to sort by using those tags is something technology is really suited to.

The flexibility of the system also makes it very practical for planning and playing. The physical mechanics, whether in analogue or digital, mean you can endlessly arrange and rearrange information without having to cross anything out or rewrite it. And if you are a visually-driven thinker, then being able to see ideas laid out and move them around so they are laid out differently will allow you to work with your brain in a way that others systems can't (yet: virtual and augmented reality offers lots of possibilities).

You can use many of the same techniques as you would with a commonplace book to make it easy for you to find the card you want to. Stickers, drawings, headings, different coloured inks and underlinings. All make things stand out. And of course as well as having a master card index, you can store different categories in different boxes making the storage of your information when you are not using it as handy as the flexibility when you are.

There are many other ways of noting down, storing, and organizing information. I recommend you look up, for example, Tiago Forte's Second Brain and PARA methods. And that you explore the numerous digital tools that exist.

But I want to suggest that the two methods I've outlined are sufficient as a starting point for you to figure out the kind of method most likely to work for you.

Both of these methods serve the same purpose: to make it as easy as possible for you to use the information you learn. And both the commonplace book and the zettelkasten do so by combining three elements:

1. Raw materials (ideas, which you have suitably primed using the techniques outlined elsewhere in this book);
2. Structure, which organizes those raw materials in ways that make them easier to deploy in response to problems; and
3. Technique(s) for manipulating ideas in relation to each other; to the structure of your system; and to problems you want to solve.

The commonplace book's physical structure is such that your raw materials will stay in the same place, and you proceed to build, expand, and use your system by finding ways to bring structure and relation to that conglomeration of information.

The zettelkasten starts with a(n admittedly flexible) structure, into which you then bring ideas.

Which of the two systems works best for you will depend on whether your brain prefers to start with information and let structure emerge out of it; or to start with structure and let information settle into it.

The advantage of digital tools is that they enable you to do both without things proliferating or getting messy. Which most closely mirrors the way that the brain iterates between theory and the evidence on which it is built. But the way it does so can lack the immersive qualities of the analogue experience. For my brain the combination of a fixed book and dynamic drawings is the best way to allow this switching between the theory and the information.

There is one system I haven't mentioned here whose absence you may be wondering at. The mind palace (or memory palace, or method of loci) is the final level boss of all information storage systems. Used at least as far back as Simonides of Ceos in the 5th century BCE, employed by thinkers, theologians, and writers through the middle ages, repopularised by the likes of Hannibal and Sherlock, used by a new generation of competitive memory athletes, and subject of some fascinating scientific study, the mind palace is what would happen if the zettelkasten system had been devised by a committee of Busby Berkeley, P T Barnum, and Harry Houdini.

The reason it is missing here is because I have afforded it its own section of considerable length elsewhere. You can skip there now if you like.

Value Extraction

Most approaches to the creative life feel like ways to fill your life with endless fascination. They make you feel like an archivist hunting hidden truths, a renaissance polymath, or at the very least an influencer pretending they got lost on the set of *The Secret History*.

And if you watch enough (or, let's be honest) any YouTube videos about techniques for being truly creative, freeing your mind, your time, your ideas, your potential, you will actually feel only one thing. Inadequate. These, you will feel, are people who lead such different lives from you that you simply can't relate.

Of course, like most people offering advice on social media, many of them do lead very different lives from you. Yes, they may have worked very hard and used exactly these techniques to do what they say they did. But the fact they had the time, space, and resources to do so usually comes from one of a number of factors that get mentioned less often. Like a supportive family, friends who let them couch surf, a lack of debt or commitment when they start out. Or finding the right niche at the right point in time to find people willing to pay. This is one reason I spend so much time in my previous book, *Living in Longhand*, explaining how to ground your goals and the methods you use to pursue them in your own life.

Back to this very particular problem. The systems I have outlined so far for keeping tabs on your projects are great. But the idea you will get to spend your life as a person of letters, flitting meaningfully between those projects, is not grounded in most people's reality.

Let's face it, most people's reality will make it hard to spend the time needed to create and maintain a zettelkasten.

Fortunately, the very best way of priming your knowledge, indeed using your knowledge, so it's ready for you to use to tackle the questions that matter to you most, is one you can employ every day. Because it involves how you do the things you have no option but to do on a daily basis.

Value extraction has kept me from sinking more than any other technique.

Poor mental health, burnout from undiagnosed neurodivergence (and the impecunity that goes with both of those) mean I have always had a "day job." I am first drafting this segment on value extraction at 7.24 in the evening at the same desk and on the same keyboard I was using until an hour ago to answer the end of day emails for that day job (and am now second editing it at the same desk at 6.23pm; and now proof reading at 6.49 on a third evening in the same place). It's not a day job I particularly enjoy, and I'm not particularly good at it: certainly not as good as I am at being creative, the thing I love most.

In all of those things, I imagine I am like many if not most of you. And if you're like me, the fact that you rely for the roof over your head and the food on your table on a day job you can do less well and that you enjoy less than the thing you care most about, the thing you know you could do that would make the biggest positive impact on the world: that drives you to the edge of a mental cliff.

The way I have kept from falling over that cliff edge is by treating my day job as a raw material. I find ways to make the tasks I perform there serve me in the parts of my life I want to improve. To use a crude analogy, my day job is a natural landscape I have bought the rights to, and I strip mine it for materials I can then use to build amazing things.

In short, there are things you have to do that feel like they are stealing hours of your life. But you have no choice other than to do those things. So why not get the most from them? Why not take every opportunity you are presented with to practise skills, methods, approaches on the day job (or unavoidable tasks like your banking or bill paying) which you can then use on your projects?

Obvious examples of how to extract value in this way include things like getting really good at spreadsheets; learning enough code (or how to use a no code platform; or, increasingly, AI) to automate tasks or generate templates.

I've used my day job to practise journaling for better productivity. And time blocking. And how to identify the most important steps in any process following the 80/20 principle and double down on those, eliminating less efficient and more time consuming steps. I've practised efficient, action-oriented minute taking, and writing committee papers and briefs for maximum impact.

When evening comes and I switch modes, I can then use those skills to squeeze every second from the few hours I have left in the day to build a business.

Volunteer for training whenever possible for the same reason. Put yourself forward to do things you've not done before, or things you're uncomfortable with: whether that's building a database, giving a talk, or organizing the ingredients in the cupboard of the coffee shop where you're a barista.

Find better ways of doing those things. Analyse, iterate, and document those ways as you go. And then transfer your new skills across in order to advance your projects.

Not only does this kind of value extraction help your projects progress, it is, more to the point here, an inherently creative pursuit. You are literally taking something from one context, its "proper place" and moving it to another, more interesting one.

Exercise 11: The Value of Anything

The aim of this exercise is to identify how you can best extract value from the things that you have to do regularly; and to determine how you can use that value for the things you want to do better or more of in life.

What one thing do you do on a regular basis that you hate having to do?

Break that thing down into its constituent tasks to create a list.

Is there one task on that list that you could use to develop skill?

What other activity (one you really want to pursue) could you apply that skill to?

Might there be a way that developing that skill could enable you to help other people solve a problem? Might other people be willing to pay you to solve that problem for them? Or to teach them how to develop the skill themselves?

Once you have identified that skill, the first thing to do is to be clear in your head why you are going to focus on it. What is the thing you really want to do with it? Try to find a way to use the skill for that purpose on a regular basis, so that you see the reward and not just the drudgery of doing it in your daily routine. This will also make the routine something you dread less, maybe even something where the progress you see creates an element of reward or satisfaction in itself. Because you will know that what you are doing in the day job will reap dividends after hours.

Next, establish a plan for improving the skill. Read about it. Find training. Measure and record progress.

Building a Palace for the Mind

At some stage, all books, articles, presentations, and films about the mind lead here. To the mind palace, or memory palace as it is also known. And while mind palaces are mainly used as a technique for memory, they were once much more than this. And they can be again, improving our creativity alongside our memory.

The rich and fascinating story of the memory palace belongs elsewhere. If you want to learn more, please go and devour Mary Carruthers' *The Book of Memory* and Frances Yates' *The Art of Memory* for a wonderful insight into the ancient Greek and mediaeval European origins of the memory palace.

But this book has the title it does for a reason. I am a theologian by training. But I am not one so obsessed that I would randomly spray around the word "monk" without any context. As many of you will know, there is a long and rich lineage of learning and cultural cutting edge in the Christian monastic tradition. Monasteries were places that housed libraries, and the scribes who copied and maintained the manuscripts that filed them.

Those libraries ensured the survival of ideas and traditions that would have long died without them. And the monks entrusted with the task of preserving this history were not only its copyists and curators but also absorbed the skills and spiritualities contained within many of those works. Memory was a key part of a cultural world in which the materials and methods of writing were expensive and labour-intensive. But there was also a deep spiritual significance to memory in a culture that revolved around the concepts both of revelation (which needed to be remembered and disseminated) and secret knowledge (to be remembered and passed down away from prying eyes).

Memory mattered. It was sacred. And its techniques were also spiritual exercises, providing pathways for the mind to follow from the physical world in which many monks believed they were unwilling captives to the spiritual world to which they aspired. Memory techniques were the ladders from the mundane to the divine.

But these memory techniques were not just about preserving knowledge. They were about producing new knowledge, expanding horizons. Finding ways for the mind to sort among and travel between ideas allowed these mediaeval and early modern thinkers to turn ancient ideas outwards to a contemporary world, to arrange and structure old wisdom and new discovery into powerful messages that would keep the traditions they cherished relevant and alive.

That is to say, at its most simple level, the memory techniques we have inherited from these monks were as much about creating a new knowledge as preserving the old.

And two monks in particular developed these techniques in ways that memory artists of today would recognise and revere.

The Franciscan Ramon Llull and the Dominican Giordano Bruno lived three and a half centuries apart. Llull's remarkable, intricate, and innovative "memory wheels" represent the pinnacle of sophisticated techniques. Bruno, whose mind palaces most contemporary memorists would find familiar, stands at a fascinating point in the history of ideas, on the cusp of one of the most important transitions for the human imagination in the West, as systems based on the flex and flow of sensory stimulation gave way to those based on the structure of verbal language. When Bruno was burned at the stake in 1600 for heresies that included accusations of magic not unrelated to his teachings on memory, it would be wrong to say this was the moment his techniques died with him, but his violent death is nonetheless a potent and timely symbol of a fundamental transition.

Before we dive into the detail, it is important to understand why the mind palace helps our creativity as well as our memory.

From Cabbies to Nobel Prizes: the Neuroscience of Creativity (Part 1)

And that brings us to another of the "M"s of the title. The MRI (specifically the fMRI or functional magnetic resonance imaging). fMRI machines are metal tubes that surround a human with giant circular magnets that allow a complete 3D image of the body to be taken. Those images capture activity within the body over time as a moving film. For neuroscientists studying the brain, this provides key information about which parts of the brain are active and when as someone carries out individual, or sequences of, tasks.

Some fascinating experiments carried out in this way hint at a physiological component to the way the mind palace enhances not just memory but creativity.

I don't want to imply anything as simplistic as saying that building and using a mind palace is some kind of biohack to reshape your brain and make you super creative.

But these experiments show that the brain is more physiologically adaptable than we might think. That is, we really can change the actual stuff inside our skulls by what we experience as mental activity. The term for this adaptability is neuroplasticity.

And the particular neuroplasticity we see at work suggests at least the possibility that using mind palaces to boost our memory might also help our brains generate new ideas.

It all starts, like so many of the best movies, with a cab ride.

One of the most famous of all brain experiments was a study of London's black cab drivers. What sets these drivers apart is the level of training they are required to undertake before they receive their license. You will (far more frequently in the days before private hire and ride sharing became so ubiquitous) regularly see people on small mopeds peppering the streets of London, their gaze flicking intently up and down between the labyrinth around them and a large folded map straddling their handlebars.

They are training to pass one of the world's most rigorous entrance exams. "The Knowledge", as it is known, takes around 3 to 4 years of this perpetual route learning to master before the test. That's about the same time as a university degree.

To pass The Knowledge, prospective black cab drivers must learn the London A to Z by heart. And not just learn it, but learn it sufficient that they can use it to navigate, in their heads, between any two points (and via any specified waymarkers) by the quickest route accounting for all the one way systems and known congestion hot spots.

It is the perfect example of "learning for use." So perfect that were there no practical application, you could imagine it had been devised and distilled over countless iterations by someone determined to find the perfect tool for practical learning.

So, with that much concentrated effort at deep work, and with that perfect a fit between technique and application, you would expect the brains of black cab drivers to have some kind of unique quality that suits them for creativity, right?

If that rhetorical structure led you to believe I was actually about to puncture your expectation by saying, "No, their brains are no different from anyone else's" then I very much hope you will enjoy my next book in this series, which is all about how to communicate ideas in order to get the reaction you want!

Because actually yes, there is something very special about the brains of black cab drivers. And what is really interesting is that their brains don't start out that way. Those years of training The Knowledge shape them.

Specifically, what Eleanor Maguire and a team from University College London showed[6] that the higher amount of grey matter cab drivers had in the brain's hippocampus at the end of their training was directly a result of their doing "The Knowledge."

She did this by a very clever use of control subjects. The team knew there was something about the brains of cab drivers that was different. And they knew that this difference coincided with their undertaking cabbie training. But, as the saying goes, correlation is not causation. There are several things that could have explained the development of this difference in the brain. Might it be, for example, that driving, rather than navigating, through the streets of London was the cause? To help figure this out, Maguire's team carried out a parallel set of experiments on control subjects consisting of another group that suddenly found itself spending more time driving round the streets of London.

What Maguire found was that, unlike those of cab drivers, the brains of trainee bus drivers didn't change. She concluded that it wasn't the act of driving that, er, drove the change. The secret sauce was the one thing that bus drivers, with their journeys that were pre-specified and part of a small finite set of possible routes repeated day after day, did not do that cab drivers did: learning to internalise maps so that you could navigate between any points on them. That is, "learning for use."

Nearly two decades later, another team of neuroscientists, at Radboud University in the Netherlands, found similar results produced in the barons of another group of individuals, who had also undertaken a very particular kind of training over a substantial period of time[7].

Boris Konrad is a memory athlete. He has won the World Memory Championship team title 8 times and appeared on TV countless times, including winning the German game show Deutschlands Superhirn (Germany's Superbrain). I highly recommend finding him on YouTube.

---
[6] https://www.pnas.org/doi/full/10.1073/pnas.070039597
[7] https://www.cell.com/neuron/fulltext/S0896-6273(17)30087-9

He also has a doctorate from the Max Planck Institute for Psychiatry on the neuronal foundations of exceptional memory performance. And he collaborated with Martin Dresler at the University of Radboud to carry out research using fMRI techniques to discover what effects memory training had on the brain. The technique they researched is the one we are looking at here. The memory palace.

They took untrained people split them into 3 groups. One group undertook no training. They had another group undertake 30 minutes of training each day for 40 days (I would love to know why 40 days–the theologian in me would like to think this is a sly nod to the traditional period of withdrawal into the desert to undergo reflection and transformation) using the memory palace technique. And, in a bid to find a control group similar to Maguire's bus drivers, they had a third group train their memory for a similar time using focused concentration (basically trying really hard to remember things, but without using any technique to link images and places).

Can you guess what the results showed? This time, the answer really is the one my words might lead you to expect. Those who trained using concentration improved their results slightly. Those who used the memory palace technique improved their results greatly. And that latter group was the only one whose brains had actually changed during the process. The research found increased activity in the hippocampus just as had been triggered by training for The Knowledge.

And they found more. What training with the mind palace produced was a greater amount of activity that connected different parts of the brain. It quite literally made people form more connections.

That's pretty remarkable. And really cool. It shows that an ancient technique to develop your memory can actually reshape the basic structure of your brain, as well as being highly effective at the task in hand.

It can make you better at learning new things, and the very particular kind of learning that creativity relies on: "learning for use."

But that's not the final piece of the puzzle.

For that, we turn to another expert on the brain.

Nancy Andreasen has the rather fabulous distinction of being the world's foremost expert on the brain structure and activity of creative genius. She led the team that carried out the delightfully-named "Iowa Study of Creative Genius[8]."

This study was designed to find out what was going on in the barons of creative people when they were being creative. It was set up, as Dresler and Maguire's were, using fMRI scans, but builds on a lot of previous work. I highly recommend reading Andreasen's paper cited in the footnote above for that background, which has some fabulous insights including a section on the relation between creativity and chaos theory which outlines a theoretical question that utterly fascinates me, asking whether creativity is an emergent property from increasingly complex systems.

In short, in order to find out what happens in the brains of creative people, the study looks at a phenomenon called, appropriately, REST. This stands for Random Episodic Silent Thought. In lay terms, it's when we let our minds wander, what I would call active pondering, and you might recognised as reflection on or teasing out of a problem or a question, playing around in your head and seeing what happens.

Andreasen knew from previous work that during REST, areas in the brain's association cortices are active. What she wanted to study was how the brain arrived at what people describe as creative insight, those flashes when key connections occur. Was there, she wondered, something different about the process in the brains of creative people?

---

[8] https://www.ncbi.nlm.nih.gov/pmc/articles/PMC3115302/

Of course, the creative brain doesn't work to order. At least, not on significantly important problems over significantly short timescales to enable an fMRI scan to capture the equivalent of Einstein realising that mass and energy are related. So she devised two proxies, both of which will be familiar to anyone who has taken part in a creative thinking exercise, whether as part of a formal test or just an office away day. She gave subjects a word and a picture, and asked them to think, quietly, about associations with that word and picture (think "uses for a paperclip").

Her subjects weren't just any group of people, as the title of the study suggests. She had a group of regular people. And two further groups. One made up of highly creative people from the artistic sphere. The other of highly creative people from scientific fields. As she puts it rather casually, the measure of highly creative was "functional." That is to say, participants were Nobel Prize winners, Fields Medalists, and Pulitzer Prize winners.

Did she find differences between people's brains during REST?

Absolutely she did. Specifically, she found significantly higher levels of activity in the association cortices of the creative groups when compared to the non-creative. And at least as interesting, she found no significant difference between the artists and scientists. Which, if the definition of creativity this book adopted right at the start, as being simply and without further detail or qualification "coming up with new things" i right, is exactly what we would expect. It's not that one area is creative and another not (the tired old "left brain/right brain" line). Rather creativity is a general (soft) skill that can manifest itself across any and all areas.

And the conclusion she drew (albeit a preliminary and tentative one)?

"The creative process is characterised by flashes of insight that arise from unconscious reservoirs of the mind and brain. Imaging studies indicate that these reservoirs reside in association cortices. During the creative process, the brain works as a self-organising system."

I'm not going to get over-excited and make scientific claims threading these three studies together with a headline like, "five minutes a day in your mind palace could make you the next Einstein." Though I eagerly await further studies, which I expect to close the gaps between these with observations from imaginative experiments.

But offering these three studies is the scientific flip side to the art I will describe in the next section. The first two show our brain's remarkable neuroplasticity, our ability to change the structure of our brain so that it does more of what we want it to do through training. The last shows that something unique happens inside the brain during the creative process. The first two hint very strongly that when it comes to "learning for use," the techniques that scholars and seekers have known about for millennia actually reshape the brain so that it can both encode and then use a vast array of information more effectively.

Could it be that the mind palace techniques practised and perfected over thousands of years might also reshape brains to promote greater levels of activity in the association cortex during REST? That is certainly the 21st century neuroscientific way of articulating what Giordano Bruno was trying to articulate in the very different (but equally state of the art) vocabulary of the Renaissance.

An Explanation and Short but Colourful Edited History of the "Method of Loci"?

The mind palace is one form of the ancient art of memory known as the "method of loci." Loci is the plural of the Latin word "locus," meaning place.

The basic principle of the method of loci is that to remember something unfamiliar or new you should associate it with something familiar. Those familiar things are the "loci" of the name.

The most famous ancient versions of this system, which apparently dates back two and a half thousand years to Simonides of Ceos, and is outlined by Cicero in his *Ad Herennium*, use a public space to provide these places.

The groundwork for learning the system is to learn to navigate, in your head, around a series of places. In ancient times, these might have been pillars in the marketplace. Students of the art would regularly pace around such marketplaces memorising the architecture so that they could later recall it effortlessly. This, of course, sounds rather like the cab drivers we looked at in the previous section. And were either the ancient Roman students of rhetoric or contemporary London cab drivers to find themselves displaced thousands of years and hundreds of miles, they would certainly have recognised a kinship with each other.

This series or collection of places is what we refer to as a mind palace, memory palace, or memory journey. If you know not only the objects or places (loci) in this palace, but are familiar with moving around and between them in an order that feels natural. This could be moving clockwise around the objects in a room, or literally moving in a line between landmarks on a journey. The purpose knowing the order in which the loci occur in your palace or journey is not just to make it easier to locate the things you want to memorise in a particular place, but to enable you to memorise sequences of things (such as a deck of cards, rulers of a country in chronological order, or the digits of Pi).

The second element of the method of loci consists of images. These represent the things to be learned, and were attached, in sequential order if that's what was required, to the places in a person's mind palace. In order to make these images more memorable, students of memory are encouraged to give them certain qualities. They should be vivid in their detail, exaggerated where possible, personalised in a way that makes them uniquely memorable to you, and ideally animated, for example having a dog wag its tail, or Archimedes jump naked out of the bath.

Strong images you have spent time working on, combined with familiar places, make for effective memory.

This method was passed down from Cicero and entered into the practice of the Dominican order of monks, of whom Giordano Bruno was, at the beginning, one.

But this tried and tested "image plus place" method of memorising was not the only path the technique took through history. Various occult and secret groups adapted it to their purposes over the years, replacing the loci of the marketplace and journey with charts of the stars or orders of angels. These could serve the same purpose of acting as hooks for helping with memory. But the studied learning of these charts and orders could also drift into contemplation of the things being learned, which in turn leaned into meditation or magic.

One practitioner of this more edgy variant of the art, who may have encountered it during his stay with the Franciscan monastic order (the differing strains of monasticism and their influences, ideas, and internecine rivalries is a truly fascinating rabbit hole if you are still looking for one, and was popularised in Umberto Eco's novel *The Name of the Rose*, turned into a film starring a pre-Heathers Christian Slater, a

Salieri-era F Murray Abraham, and Sean Connery sporting a truly unapologetic accent), was Ramon Llull.

Rather than a memory journey or palace, Llull is best known for his memory wheels. These were formed from concentric circles. The outer circle contained significant letters or words, representing divine attributes or spiritual qualities. The inner wheels contained similar symbols, representing different levels in the hierarchies of similar objects. The inner wheels could be turned. The purpose of this was to help people move from the earthly to the spiritual, using each successive circle as a step on a ladder. But it was also to help form connections, to help understand the connectedness of all things, and to see how eternal properties could manifest in many ways ("goodness," for example could apply in its own way to the goodness of God or the goodness of a season, the goodness of a person, or the goodness of an apple).

It is, as Frances Yates says of Llull's system in her seminal book *The Art of Memory*, very hard for the modern mind to quite grasp what he was trying to do. We do know that it fitted within a long esoteric tradition, and a belief in the way the world is ordered on levels from the immaterial to the divine.

Most significantly for us, Llull had managed to build fluidity into the very structure of his memory techniques.

He created a system in which movement was expected and normal and in which there was no such thing as a "proper place" for ideas. Their proper place was wherever they served the most useful purpose.

If the Ciceronian tradition was multisensory but static, Llull's was conceptual but fluid.

For the memory palace to become the engine for creativity that is about both knowing lots about lots and joining all that knowledge together (the purpose we want it to serve), what was needed was a fusion of these two traditions.

Enter Giordano Bruno.

Giordano Bruno is one of the most celebrated and colourful characters of the early modern age. Living through the end of the 16th century, his early life overlapped the end of Michelangelo's and his later life the early years of Galileo (who was born in the year Michelangelo died, 1564). He has captured the public imagination so much that he is the subject of S J Parris' bestselling series of historical crime novels.

Although he started out as a Dominican monk (where he will have encountered Cicero's memory palace techniques) in Italy, he is the archetype of what we think of as a Renaissance man, who travelled widely through Europe, both spreading what he had learned so far, and learning new things as he travelled.

It was not long before he had also absorbed Llull's wheel-based system. His own memory techniques, which he spread far and wide as he travelled, including during a celebrated stay in my home city of Oxford, did more than just fused these two traditions. They, as Frances Yates puts it, represent, "an extreme 'occultizing' of both the classical art and Lullism.[9]"

The method of loci became, for Bruno, a way of learning and storing secret wisdom, and the wheels of Llull became a way of harnessing celestial power and internalising it in the imagination.

This may sound like so much esoteric speculation, that has little to do with the science of the MRI we have just been talking about. But Bruno inhabited the same courts and

---

[9] Art of Memory, p 208

intellectual gatherings in the same curious world at the same time as the great alchemists like John Dee. Historians of science have come to realise that much of the experimental method pioneered by those alchemists paved the way for much of modern science intellectually, experimentally, and very practically by raising the appetite of those in charge of the purse strings needed to fund laboratories. Not to mention more widespread attention coming to the alchemical interests of those we think of as actual founders of modern science like Isaac Newton. In the same way, the occultists of memory were very much the methodological forebears of our modern understanding and practice of creative problem solving.

The alchemists sought to transform one substance into another, and in doing so gave birth to what we would recognise as experimental chemistry. Bruno sought to transform one kind of idea into another, and in doing so paved the way for the use of the imagination in framing hypotheses, understanding paradigm shifts, solving problems by thinking outside the parameters in which they arose, and systems thinking.

As well as being the direct ancestor of so many valuable creative techniques, what Bruno captured in his attempt to relate the heavenly and the earthly through the art of memory was the fundamental relation between imagination and impact. He understood that to change the world you must first change how you think. And he identified the ancient art of memory as critical to that change. He linked memory and creativity, through imagination as trained using a method we would recognise as belonging to the tradition of the mind palace.

And that brings us right back to you. And the importance of building your own mind palace. Not just so that you can use it to help memorise a deck of cards in order to impress your friends. Though that's both fun and great mental training. But so that you have a way of storing your ideas that will enable your imagination to use them as rocket fuel for creative problem solving.

So let's bring all of that together and start building.

Building Your Own Palace of the Mind

At this point, a quick aside. When people talk about memory in general, and the mind palace technique in particular, they often talk about mental images. Each locus, for example, is characterised as a picture in your mind's eye of a particular place. But that can be unhelpful. First, not everyone is able to experience mental pictures. Aphantasia is the term that describes this lack of mental imagery. Several percent of the population is aphantasic. I talk more about this in a later section of this book about mental imagery. But the lack of actual mental pictures in your head doesn't necessarily mean that you can't build a mind palace. It will just be one that works on terms you are familiar with.

Second, mental imagery is too limiting. What matters is involving the senses—not just one of them. Internal sensory landscape is probably more what we mean when we use the shorthand "mental image".

Anthony Metivier, an expert memory teacher of today, explains both of these points well and in greater detail[10]. I also recommend him as a guide if you want to devote a considerable time to building your own memory palaces and using them for memorisation.

What follows will serve you well should you want to start on the path to improving your memory. But it is intended specifically to help you build a memory palace as a tool for your creative journey.

---

[10] https://www.magneticmemorymethod.com/memory-palace/

Creating the architecture

A memory palace has, as we saw in the outline above, two basic elements. There are places, and there are images. Places are the structural architecture of the palace designed to help you store and use your knowledge. Images are the objects representing that knowledge, the things with which you fill the empty structure.

The key to the success of your memory palace as a creative tool is how you build and arrange two elements. More than two thousand years of tradition has seen a few fundamental techniques emerge on which almost everyone agrees. The use of your senses, can be applied to both images and places. Familiarity and order are mainly for your places, movement mainly for your images, as is exaggeration, though that can also apply to your places.

These elements aren't magic. And they aren't random. They are all there with the intention of making things more, well, memorable. If you spend a little time considering each you will soon realise that already the things you remember best are ones that have some or more of these features.

But where do you start building a memory palace?

Contemporary memory athletes will have many of them, small enough to learn quickly. This means they can, for example, memorise many decks of cards using a different palace or journey for each deck to avoid any confusion. Building multiple smaller journeys or palaces can be a great way to learn, even if the ultimate aim is to create one larger "master." You could, later, incorporate these smaller elements into something larger.

When it comes to the format of your master memory palace itself, you could start with something you know really well. It doesn't have to be a building. It could be a map of an area, whether that's a county whose towns you know well or a park whose landmarks you visit regularly. Or it could be a long, familiar journey with lots of memorable waymarkers such as the commute to work or college, a favourite walk or a high street in your hometown.

Or you can use a building. One of the most famous memory palace users in fiction is Hannibal Lecter. Thomas Harris goes into great detail describing Lecter's mental creation in the novel Hannibal, and tells us that Lecter based the design of his memory palace on the Topkapi Palace in Istanbul. I have the great fortune to be based in Oxford and that gives me access to some of the most beautiful large buildings in the world. As a result my own memory palace is based on the Ashmolean Museum and parts of the old Bodleian Library, and I get to spend hours at a time wandering through ancient artefacts and antique books in the name of training.

One point worth bearing in mind is to limit the extent to which the different areas of your mind palace are removed from each other. The structure should follow the Aristotelian principle of unity of place. That is to say, you should have a single site where each area flows freely into others. If your mind needs to "jump" at any point then it's easy to get lifted out of your concentration. That's not to say that you shouldn't be able to transport from one side of the palace to another. Indeed creative flexibility would benefit from that. But if you use cities on a map as your basic structure, then the highways between those cities require you to make regular imaginative leaps that are harder than, say, moving through a door to get from one area to the next. Of course, the real test in practice will, as always, be finding something that works for you.

It's all very well having a skeleton outline, but your mind palace will only start becoming useful once you start to fill it. And it can be incredibly daunting knowing what to keep where when there is, quite literally, a whole world of choice staring you down.

I recommend you start with the knowledge map you created in an earlier exercise. This will give you plenty of content. But it will also give you a starting point for deciding which subjects should be where in relation to each other.

Using (all) your senses

Your memory palace itself, and the information you store inside it, should be as vivid as you can possibly make it.

The first way you can do this is by using as many of your senses as you possibly can to make everything feel as real as possible when you spend mental time there.

When it comes to reproducing our senses in thought, the sense we often think of first is sight. Common vocabulary shows us this. We have phrases such as "the mind's eye" and "mental imagery" but no corresponding "the mind's ear" or "mental smellery."

And creating the most vivid and detailed visual imagery you can is important. For most sighted people, the primary sense we use to navigate the physical world is sight. So it makes sense that we should do the same in the mental world we are building. Sight enables us to focus on a particular object or zoom in on a specific part of an object. (As an aside, it would be fascinating to think about creating a mind palace as it might be used by an echo-locating bat, a rodent that steers by its whiskers, or a shark or elephant with an incredibly sharp sense of smell).

To assist in adding detail to your mind palace and the information you store, practise being an observer. You can of course do this with other senses, but with sight, and also sound, it is much easier to keep a record of your observations through photographs, sound recording, and film. Keep pictures or clips of things you want to use in your mind palace. Take photos as you go about your life. But don't use taking photos or film as a replacement for studying the details of what you are capturing. Instead use technology to enhance your senses, revisiting and refreshing the experiences you have.

But also add other senses. In Thomas Harris' novels, Hannibal Lecter's primary sense is smell. This is partly an effort on Harris' part to create a feeling that Lecter is somehow primal, an ancient, archetypal monster slightly removed from humanity, who for all his intellectualisation is still dependent on something old and dark.

But it's also because smell is one of the most effective senses we have for evoking memory. One of the reasons the opening line of Gabriel García Marquéz's novel *Love in the Time of Cholera* is so powerful is that so many of us will recognise the strength of its connection between a particular smell and a powerful emotional memory we associate with that smell:

"It was inevitable: the scent of bitter almonds always reminded him of the fate of unrequited love."

One of the most interesting projects I ever took part in as a writer was the Arts Council Funded collaboration Penning Perfumes[11] which brought together a group of poets and a group of perfumiers. Half of the poets wrote verse based on a smell they had been sent by a perfumier, and half of the perfumiers created scents based on a poem written for them. This kind of cultural exchange can not only produce really interesting results. It can expand the creative horizons of all who take part.

Do for smell the same as for sight. Try to spend some time next time you go for a walk actively noticing the many different smells and the things associated with them. Make them raw materials for your mind palace. Stop by hedgerows and learn to distinguish honeysuckle from jasmine from wisteria. Start noticing the smells of different shops, of foods and drinks, of fabric conditioners, soaps (and yes, some of the less pleasant ones, too): expand your olfactory vocabulary!

---

[11] https://sabotagereviews.com/2013/03/12/review-penning-perfumes-oxford-210213/

Do the same with your other senses. And make an effort as you create rooms in your mind palace to incorporate all of those senses. If you are literally using a palace, include the kitchen and washrooms, have a music room, make the floors and walls and surfaces different textures, notice whether the windows of some rooms are open letting in birdsong and the smell of climbing plants (or the sounds and smells of the city!).

Movement and Exaggeration

Sensory details are just one way of making things memorable. Things are more likely to grab your attention and stick in your mind if you add movement, exaggeration, or humour.

Have objects interact with each other and with the things around them. Turn all the dials up to 11, whether that's making clothes intensely bright, giving someone really large teeth, or having a robin start whistling its song through a megaphone.

Don't be shy, don't be embarrassed. Don't tell yourself something is inappropriate (we will look at techniques to help you get over this natural tendency to self-censor in the next section). Just remember that (at least until Neuralink is a long way down the line) your memory palace is yours and yours alone. No one else can access your places or your images. No one else ever need know what they are. So have at it! Be as NSFW, as cringingly cheesy, or as blatantly out of kilter with your public persona as you wish!

And use emotion. Most people who teach the art of memory stress the importance of humour (see my earlier comment about giving people large teeth or having a robin whistle through a megaphone).

Less is said about other emotions. Some emotions can dull the mind for many people, or sidetrack it, or take it down paths we don't want to go down. But experiment. If particular emotions help you to remember things, then use them. Find what works for you.

If you're like me, you will find yourself wandering as you build. It's like sorting through boxes of old stuff you find in the attic. It seemed like a small and simple job in the morning but you suddenly find it's dinner time and nothing's got done because you were too busy reading through old diaries and cards from Aunt Hilda's holiday in Jerez, which sent you to a website on the history of sherry production and down a rabbit hole of barrel making and imagining Aunt Hilda stowing away bootleg cargo on the ferry home and having to bribe her way past customs with a keg of olive oil (which was rarer when she travelled, which you know because you couldn't help skipping over to that part of Wikipedia).

If you find that happening, for goodness' sake let it! That's not a distraction. It's practice!

Familiarity and Order

In the ancient world, there were some fairly strict rules about the spacing of the objects in the structure of your memory palace. It was considered important for there to be plenty of what architects might call negative space. And objects should be evenly spaced. The former ensures your memory palace isn't cluttered. You should be able to distinguish between different areas. The latter ensures, in accordance with the principle of unity we mentioned above, that your mind never has to struggle to reach the next landmark: they keep coming in a rhythm.

Strict rules might be too prescriptive, but those principles are well made. They make the recall of information much easier.

These final two properties also serve that purpose. Your memory palace should be based on something that is familiar to you, and will continue to be familiar to you until it is imprinted on your mind. That's why many people use buildings or journeys from their daily life rather than creating fantasy castles or mansions. It might sound wonderful to create something wholly new, something that lets your wildest imagination run riot.

But that kind of fantasy will usually lack the depth or the detail of something really familiar. And your memory palace needs a lot of detail. Enough to house, at least at a high level, everything you know. In each "room" or area, you will be storing many different pieces of information. Each piece or at least each group of information will need to be connected to its own distinctive feature within that room. So rather than just knowing that a room is spacious and beautiful, with wooden floors and a high ceiling, you need to know details such as the furniture, what's on the table, what ornaments are on the mantelpiece and so on.

And knowing that level of detail about your memory palace will help you create structure for your knowledge. You will then be able easily to navigate and explore, to summon a particular idea and to take it for a walk, play with it, move it and see how it might make friends with other ideas it encounters on a tour.

Once the information in your memory palace has a home, once you know where to find it when you need it, you can move it around at will. If you find yourself on the roof and think, "Ooh, I could just do with something from the basement," you should be able to fetch it and bring it back effortlessly. If you are wandering through a gallery devoted to the science of rivers and see something that reminds you of commuters emptying from the subway at night, you should be able to go straight to the room where you store what you know about the movement of crowds or the rhythms of cities, and see whether the connection you made has any mileage.

I often refer to this when I'm teaching as "building a mind palace with leaky plumbing." A more accurate way might be to think of every "place" in your memory palace as a point on a circuit board connected to every other place by materials that offer no impedance.

Exercise 12: Build your own mind palace.

No surprise what the exercise for this section is. Of course, you're not going to build a memory palace the size of a sprawling metropolis in a few minutes. Or hours. Or days. But you can start, maybe using your knowledge map as a base, and the techniques outlined in this section. And as you build, you can begin to furnish your places with images. Take your time. Learn what works for you. This is an exercise that will be with you for the rest of your life.

Joining the Dots

Memory palaces, especially in their role in the art of Giordano Bruno, are the bridge between learning and creativity. They exist to store and to organise information, but to do so in a way that keeps that information in a state of permanent readiness, ready to be deployed in service of creating new ideas, new solutions to old problems.

Ready for us to start forming new connections.

Which brings us seamlessly to another fascinating set of fMRI experiments

All that jazz: The Neuroscience of Creativity (Part 2)

One of the things we have talked about several times in this book is the annoying tendency of our brains to prevent us from travelling down truly creative paths. Our "self-censor" is our creativity's worst enemy. We all know that. And yet, no matter how few people we know are privy to our innermost thought experiments about a maple syrup island in the shape of a giant mallard, populated by purple notebooks perpetually singing Jedward lyrics in Tibetan, every time we start to wander that way our brains say no.

The second ingredient in creativity is joining the dots between all our newly installed and primed points of knowledge. But to join the dots truly creatively we need to get rid of that self-censor. Or at least, to misquote the adverts of my youth from a well-known energy supplier, to make it "turn off and onable."[12]

So how do we do this? Where would we start looking for clues?

---

[12] https://www.youtube.com/watch?v=NuIYV_4DqYo

The Monk, The Mushroom, and the MRI

It turns out one key to helping us find the answer to that question comes precisely from where we might expect it. With some of our society's most celebrated experts at shifting things out of their proper place and ignoring the voice saying, "it shouldn't be done like this": improvisers.

Neuroscientists have studied the brains of two of the most notable groups of improvisers, jazz musicians and battle rappers, to try and find out what is actually going on in their heads when they improvise, when they stop following the established repertoire and play what has never been played or say what has never been said before.

What they found provides a really helpful starting point for those of us who want to train ourselves to put the world out of joint as effortlessly as they do, to let new connections, new formulations, new ideas flow freely.

To cut straight to the chase, the exact thing at which the best improvisers excel is silencing that internal voice that says "don't go there." Something makes them able to take their minds to places the rest of us can't because they have learned how to turn off the parts of their brains that tell them not to do so.

Studies into the brains of these improvisers by Charles Limb (on jazz musicians) and Siyuan Liu (on rappers) took a very simple format. An artist was placed into a functional magnetic resonance imaging (fMRI) machine and told to start improvising. In the case of jazz, pianists were selected for the practical reason that a saxophonist or clarinettist might find it harder to operate their instrument inside an fMRI machine that surrounds the head with powerful magnets.

What happened when the improvisation started was fascinating. This is how the abstract to Limb's paper, *Neural Substrates of Spontaneous Musical Performance: An fMRI Study of Jazz Improvisation*, puts it. When improvisation began, there was:

"extensive deactivation of dorsolateral prefrontal and lateral orbital regions with focal activation of the medial prefrontal (frontal polar) cortex. Such a pattern may reflect a combination of psychological processes required for spontaneous improvisation, in which internally motivated, stimulus-independent behaviours unfold in the absence of central processes that typically mediate self-monitoring and conscious volitional control of ongoing performance. Changes in prefrontal activity during improvisation were accompanied by widespread activation of neocortical sensorimotor areas"

In lay terms, the part of the brain we associate with self-censorship, that internalised convention we talked about earlier, switched off. The parts of the brain that lit up were those parts associated with motor function. Their brains literally went on autopilot.

The key to disjointing the world seems in a very literal sense to be turning off our inner self censor. And the fact that these expert improvisers are able to perform what seems to many of us, who bend to its commands without complaint, such an impossible task suggests that it is possible to learn how to do this.

Of course, what these scientists were studying is correlation. What it is that happens in the brain when certain things happen. We cannot deduce from this alone what causes these changes. But we can look at the practice of practice as it were in these fields, for some clues as to how their brains might have acquired these neural correlates to the finished art.

Deliberate Practice

A hint to at least one of the key elements in this training is the fact the motor parts take over from it during improvisation. What this suggests is that a certain level of technical fluency is required. Our brains need to be really good at operating the mechanical system. The playing of an instrument, the delivery of lines, must be so proficient that it *can* be automatic. This is something anyone who plays sport at an advanced level will testify to. To perform at the highest level, you must know the mechanics of what you are doing so well that you do not have to think about them at all. They take care of themselves. This enables people to get what they would call "in the zone."

And of course, it's not just sport. Think of so many of the skills we take for granted. Like driving, or riding a bicycle (having never approached mastery of either, I think I might take a sporting example over both of those!). For days and weeks, in some cases years, we perform these actions at first awkwardly. Then, though the action becomes more fluent, we remain aware of what our bodies are doing. The transition from one micro-constituent of the overall movement to another is a conscious one. From the inside it can feel as though we are talking our bodies through what they need to do.

But after hours and hours of practice over a prolonged period, more of those micro transitions become seamless. And eventually we find that we are able to complete the whole action without actively thinking about it at all. It has become automatic. It is as though responsibility for its execution has shifted from one part of the brain to another.

To learn how to achieve this "autopilot" state best across a wide variety of activities, Anders Ericsson and Robert Pool's book *Peak* is an incredibly valuable resource. I also recommend Daniel Coyle's *The Talent Code*, which goes into some more specific detail about the neurological changes that occur when you adopt their method.

What Pool and Ericsson found is that across a vast array of pursuits, the way practitioners progressed most swiftly and efficiently from the "consciously talking your body through the steps" state to the "automatic" stage was through a very particular form of deliberate practice.

That form of deliberate practice has two elements. The first is procedural. This involves first breaking down any activity you want to master into its most fundamental steps. Once you have done that, you practise each of those steps in isolation until it becomes automatic. Then you work on the transitions between each of the steps, slowly knitting more of those transitions into a seamless chain until the whole action is complete.

The second is the way that procedure is applied. This involves always working on those things that are just but only just beyond your capability. It's a method that seems counterintuitive to many of us. And it runs counter to a lot of training methods that focus on repeating drills or scales, or beginning sessions with aspects of a discipline that we already know well.

In this section we will take a look at those actions specific to forming connections that you can attempt to master using this kind of deliberate practice.

Learning to Turn Off Your Self-Censor

But first, let's go back to those jazz pianists, and the mechanics of improvisation, of turning off the inner self-censor. Because one of the keys to successful creativity will be finding a way to do what they are able to do, and let the ideas flow without a part of your brain standing on the sidelines and tutting judgmentally at them.

One of the truisms around creativity is that schools educate creativity out of children. It's the idea at the heart of Ken Robinson's presentation *Do Schools Kill Creativity?*, for a long time the most watched TED talk ever.

In a way the answer to that question is, simply, "yes." I've held creativity workshops and events many times. The ones I enjoy the most are those I hold with members of the public drawn from across the generations. One of the things I've found to be almost an immutable law is that when children take part with their parents, they have qualitatively more originality than the grown-ups with them. Ideas just flow out of them. Before I've finished asking a question they'll be half way through the third or fourth flight of fancy. Grown-ups on the other hand are more considered. They'll think before launching in. And often they'll intervene in their child's stream of consciousness: something I always nip in the bud in no uncertain terms just as I make it very clear to both parent and child how fantastic the youngster's imagination is. So yes, grown-ups, and certainly schools are a big part of that, do teach creativity out of children.

But as so often the real answer is, "yes, but it's not quite that simple." Think of the same phenomenon from another angle. Daniel Kahneman held the notable distinction of having won the Nobel Prize for Economics despite being a psychologist. You might say he embodies the ideal of shifting things from their "proper place". He won the Nobel for his contribution to Prospect Theory, which explains why value is a relative term, but his most influential contribution to public thought is to be found in the book *Thinking Fast and Slow*.

Kahneman distinguishes the older parts, in evolutionary terms, of the brain, which "think fast" and the later-evolved "slow thinking" parts. Fast thinking can be seen in action in the way we instinctively react to possible danger. We have evolved to never miss a possible threat. Because the cost of doing so would be catastrophic. Slow thinking, on the other hand, is the more considered kind of rationalising that enabled us to develop tools and systems of evaluation of a situation's more abstract properties and possibilities. It is what makes us truly human, and it is slow because it can afford to be.

The problem with fast thinking is that by and large we no longer face daily existential peril the way our ancestors did. But our brains still react as though we did. Our fast thinking feeds our slow thinking consistently, and we do well to develop processes that recognise this influence and challenge it. The result causes anxiety, and can often stop us pursuing more fruitful paths throughout our day. Steve Peters developed this idea in sports psychology through what he calls the chimp paradox, referring to the fast thinking ancient part of our brain that hampers our progress by getting in the way of our slower more rational brains.

The solution to the overactive fast thinking parts of our brain is to dedicate ourselves to prioritising our slow thinking. To interrupt fast thought in order to allow time for careful calculation.

This strategy, of challenging and often quieting the fast brain and amplifying the slow brain, is key to surviving and evolving.

But I'm sure you see where this is going. It's not that the adults involved in helping us grow up have sabotaged creativity. It's rather that the techniques they impart to help us be more considered, less anxious, more able to get the most rational bang for our evolved brain's buck have the unfortunate side effect of making it harder for us to switch that part of our brain off when it would be really useful for us to do so. The considered and interrupting parents I come across so often want to equip their children for a world in which fast thinking that runs out of control can be catastrophic. And they succeed in that. The problem is the by-product: that it becomes harder for the brain to let go of slow thinking when it would be beneficial to do so.

The key, in other words, is not to "undo what kids learn at school." It's to enable them to reconnect with the older parts of their brain by switching off their self-censor. Not all the time, but at will, so that they slip effortlessly between the fluid and the deliberative as the situation requires. Just like the jazz musicians they need an improvisational fluidity that's turn off and onable.

Let's look at the techniques we can train, through deliberate practice, to develop that "fluidity at will."

.

Mycelium: new connections

Mycelium is the first creative thinking training tool I developed.

It emerged out of a weekend locked in my office in response to a call for competition entries for the Oxford Humanities Innovation Challenge. In reality it had been fermenting way for about 4 decades before then, from my earliest storytelling endeavours at primary school through my weekly time spent lost in the Independent's creativity puzzles, which eventually evolved into the real world of the Creative Thinking World Championship at the first ever Mind Sports Olympiad. Along the way it picked up pieces of my love of role playing games and of card games. I was an obsessive player. For the best part of a decade I played bridge for at least 12 hours a day, every day, and made it to the Great Britain under 20 and under 25 national teams. At school I organised Top Trumps tournaments (Top Trumps sets were second only to stamp catalogues in terms of places where I actually learned stuff).

And I wasn't just fascinated by playing card games. For my History A-level project, I wrote a detailed history of playing card decks in Tudor and Stuart England and their occasional tangential tangles with the political shenanigans of the time.

I was also both passionate and obsessed by the design of card decks. I've always loved beautiful design. And the playing card is the perfect canvas for beautiful design. It's small enough that you have to think incredibly carefully about what to include but not so small you can't fill it with detail. It's the perfect portable size, which means you can design it for any setting from the most personal to the most public. It should be attention catching sufficient that it instantly draws the stranger's eye but capable of being a constant companion through hours of gaming without players ever tiring or ceasing to find something new. It also perfectly combines aesthetic and purpose. Not only should its design be beautiful, it should be clear. And it should have sufficient layers of meaning for potential complex game play.

All of which is a way of saying it was inevitable that my first creative tool should be a card game. And I would highly recommend you spending some time working on your own!

How it works

Mycelium provides a structure for a very tried and tested type of creative thinking exercise in which the objective is to find new ways to connect different items. By adding game play and a rich aesthetic, the aim is to provide the same multisensory environment we saw with the mind palace and to use dopamine reinforcement to help the brain on its way.

Mycelium is a game played with two decks of cards (you can buy them from the Rogue Interrobang website or you can download a free printable pdf at https://rogueinterrobangdotcom.files.wordpress.com/2020/03/cards-front-full-66.pdf). One deck contains 16 cards that each contain a question or scenario with two blanks. At its simplest this might be something like "What do you get if you cross...with...?" Some are more complicated scenarios such as "After the zombie apocalypse you can choose to save...or...Explain your choice." The other deck contains 40 cards with an object on them.

Game play is very simple. You can of course create problems to work on by yourself. Indeed, if you are reading this book as part of a personal mission to live a more creative life, that is probably what you will do. But it is easiest to explain the principles behind it in the context of playing as a group. You take one card from the deck of 16 which gives you a semi complete question, and two from the deck of 40 to complete the question. The result will be something like:

"After the zombie apocalypse you can choose to save a potter's wheel or ants. Explain your choice."

Players have five minutes (this is arbitrary but in practice has turned out to work rather well) to come up with as many answers as they possibly can. It's really important that there are no limits on what people can say.

At the end of that time, everyone's answers are compared and scored.

You might recognise the scoring principles as the three classical elements in creative thinking: originality, elaboration, and prolificness. Every idea gets points. The number of points each idea scores depends on its originality and how well developed it is.

For originality, the more people who come up with an idea (or a variation of it), the fewer points it scores. If 10 people are playing, then an idea only one person has would score 10 points, and an idea all 10 people come up with would score 1, with all the options in between graded exactly as you would imagine so that the score equals 11 minus the number of people who have the idea. This provides a concrete reward for the original, absurd, unusual and ridiculous (encouraging dopamine to help our self-censor go away).

Additional reward is given for the degree of detail in any answer, reflecting how complex and convincing the idea is. This includes, for example, the level of world-building behind an idea, and whether that idea makes sense within this imaginary world. This is scored on a scale of 1 to 5. And that is then multiplied by the originality score to give the total for each idea. A person's overall score in a round is the sum of all their idea scores.

Going back to our sample question, you might score 1 for detail if your answer is, "I'd save the potter's wheel so I could still eat my dinner off a plate." A more elaborate answer might be, "I would save the potter's wheel so I could make plates and everyone in our post-apocalyptic community would be able to eat off plates and remember how much family meals were a part of life before the apocalypse."

A more elaborate answer still might be:

"I would save the potter's wheel to make plates. I would run workshops and gatherings with fellow survivors so we could make plates together and reminisce as we did about the times before the apocalypse and the importance of communal meals, building a small but close-knit community around these memories. I would teach people how to use the wheel as we talked and charge a small fee for each person to create their own personally made set of plates to give them a sense both of civic togetherness and individual pride at their newfound skill. As a result of both of these, and the stories about the importance of communal meals that we told as we worked, everyone would be encouraged to come for a grand feast to mark the founding of our new community around this newfound bond and skill. People would pay me a nominal fee for a seat at the table, and I would throw a celebration party. Of course, I would invite the zombies along because the real feast would be for them, and the plate-making villagers would be what was on the menu. That way I would end up with zombie allies, a pile of cash, and no rivals for any remaining resources."

There is no hard and fast rule on, say, "what a 3 looks like" when it comes to scoring originality. One of the things that helps the game enhance creativity and thinking about creativity is having these discussions afterwards and trying to agree among yourselves.

And when it comes to scoring for originality the discussions are even more part of the creative process. Just what makes two things versions of the same idea? Clearly "you could use it to hit zombies over the head" and "you could hack the zombies to pieces with it" are two versions of the "weapons" idea.

But what about the following answers to our original question:

1. "I would use the potter's wheel to make plates so that some degree of civilization would be restored even though what we were eating off them was raw zombie meat."

2. "I would use the potter's wheel to make bowls that could be traded for essential items."

3. "I would save ants because watching them as they nest and work would be a reminder of the necessary elements of civilization we needed to restore as we began to rebuild."

Which of these are "the same idea?" On the surface, 1 and 2 are both about "making pottery." On the other hand 1 and 3 are both about "restoring civilization." Or you could take that point even further and say that 1, 2, and 3 are all variations on "restoring the fundamental elements of society." Very often the discussion around these questions will not only be incredibly thought-provoking and make people do some deep thinking, but they will lead to each idea sparking lots of other ideas until the game gets lost in the general creative conversation.

Exercise 13: Icy ants

Below is another sample question. Give yourself five minutes to come up with as many ideas as you can, and give them as much detail as you can, imagining what a world might be like in which each of them occurs.

And when you're done, read on and I'll go through some of the thought processes you might follow to generate and explore ideas.

What would happen if a glacier and ants swapped places for a day?

Commentary

There are some things that might strike you straightaway about the differences between ants and a glacier. And teasing out those differences will help you start.

Ants are small and glaciers are large, for example. So imagine you were climbing across a glacier and it suddenly changed into ants. Likewise, suppose you noticed ants in the carpet at home only to suddenly find a massive moving river of ice in your sitting room.

You also tend to find them in different parts of the world. Ants might make you think of fire ants in the rainforest, for example. And glaciers tend to cluster high up and around the poles. So both ants and glaciers will find themselves in unfamiliar places–which will have interesting consequences for both them and their surroundings.

You can get to a more interesting level of idea by delving deeper into things associated with one of the two objects in a Mycelium question, and asking how it crosses over to the other.

What is it that ants do, for example? Think of the way they interact with their environment, cutting up pieces of leaf in the forest, building nests, even forming part of the food chain. To take the last point first, how might an anteater cope if it found all of a sudden when it turned up to the local feeding place that its day's snack had been replaced by a wall of ice (maybe it wouldn't be so bad. Might this be how anteaters discover a hitherto undiscovered talent with gelato?) Worse still, what if it was mid meal when the change occurred?

Next, look at things the two items you're linking already have in common. In the case of ants and a glacier, an obvious example would be the way they move slowly and relentlessly as a mass unit. Imagine a stream of ants instead of carving out a path of leafy food on the forest floor carving out the sides of a valley. What might the resulting scenery look like? How might future tourists or geologists marvel at the valley wonders? And if a glacier were suddenly to find itself sliding through the forest floor, maybe it would deposit some of the things it had already picked up on its travels. Instead of planes that go missing appearing decades later on a valley floor, they might now appear thousands of miles away cradled in jungle vines.

And finally, look at key words in the question that might give you some hints. In this case think about the part that says, "for a day." The implication is that this isn't permanent. What happens when things change back? What dreams might the ants wake up with the next morning? And what new objects might the glacier have acquired that it would deposit in the valleys in decades to come causing confusion all round?

Dan Holloway

sport	Anthropology	art	cities	physics	marine ecosystems	government	botany	cartography	deserts
exploration	Industrialisation	literature	food	space	pack animals	disease	forests	agriculture	oceans and seas
medicine	inventions	galleries	business	biology	insects	war & peace	crop plants	migration	rivers
Communication	hierarchy	live culture	politics	computing	reptiles	social systems	algae	climate	ice caps
discovery	ideology	fashion	media	maths	fish	stone age	fungi	rainforest	grassland
crime	mythology	film	advertising	medicine	birds	iron age	seeds	oceans	mountains
oppression & liberation	religion	gaming	the law	classification & measurement	mammals	prehistory	arids and alpines	plate tectonics	islands
transport	philosophy	fantasy	communities	robots	extra-terrestrial life	revolution	ocean plants	weather	land mass movement
records	futurology	horror	education	chemistry	extremophiles	archives	plants and ecosystems	taming and rewilding	natural disasters
AI	luxury	science fiction	life online	engineering	evolution & adaptation	oral history	killer plants	extinction & conservation	the cosmos

Taking Ideas for a Walk

You will recall I mentioned that when I devised Mycelium I set myself the challenge of dividing the whole of human knowledge into 100 categories. The result was the table overleaf.

We have already looked at all kinds of ways in which this was a useful exercise and how you might use it as, for example, a template or a comparator for your knowledge map.

The original purpose was to create a drafting table to enhance the game play element of Mycelium. The idea was that at the start of each round, before a question was drawn either players could choose, or someone would roll a 100 sided dice to select, a category. Any answers to whatever question was set that referenced this particular category would score double points.

But you can also use it to get you started on creating ideas more fluidly, by using it as a mental travelling companion whenever you tackle a creative challenge. It's a method I employed long before I had devised the table. And I have always called it "taking an idea for a walk."

Unlike the "random walk" that might suggest, recalling the title of Burton Malkiel's seminal book on the behaviour of stock markets[13], this is a very purposeful walk indeed.

Let me explain using the most famous creative thinking question of all.

"How many uses can you think of for a paperclip?"

When I ask this question in workshops, people tend to start off by thinking what a paperclip might look like a miniature version of. Such as an ironing board. Or a diving board. Their answer is then "A diving board for ants" and/or "an ironing board for ants." (yes, I am aware that ants are becoming a bit

---

[13] Malkiel, B. *A Random Walk Down Wall Street*, W W Norton & Co, New York, 1973

of a leitmotif. Entirely unintended, though you really should go down the rabbit hole of learning about these remarkable creatures).

Eventually, people run out of things a paperclip could be used for by ants. And they run out of things that aren't paper but a paperclip could nonetheless join together. Some wonder what they could do if they unfurled the clip into a small piece of metal. That might get you a few more things for ants to use, and several things you could skewer to make a canapé kebab. And at that point many people stop.

Approaching the question by "taking it for a walk" is a way to avoid the onset of block at this point. The exercise might go something like this. Start at a random place on the drafting table. "Rivers," for example. The question now becomes, "How could you use a paperclip in the context of rivers?" I might realise I could use a paperclip to create turbulence in an otherwise still river to help create a training facility for whitewater canoeing practice. Now I begin my "walk" by visiting another category. I might go to "music" and wonder if I could hollow the paperclip out to make a very high pitched brass instrument, for example.

And we carry on in the same way through every section.

This kind of trip through the panoply of knowledge's vaults avoids us getting stuck in a loop. The list of categories provides a set of waymarkers for subtly changing up the question. It can also prompt us to take more detailed excursions later on into some of the areas we had previously not considered.

The Monk, The Mushroom, and the MRI

Context, Constraint, and Creativity

Adding a drafting table with 100 categories of knowledge to the structure of our mental forays into connectivity illustrates two key elements of practical creativity: context and constraint.

By the influence of context on creativity I mean that when we take something familiar and transplant it to an unfamiliar area we can often see all kinds of things we hadn't previously imagined: both about the thing and its environment. When it comes to problem solving in the real world, this can work in two ways. Sometimes a problem in an area with which we are really familiar can open itself up when we explore it from a totally new angle. And sometimes our expertise in one area can enable us to see answers to problems in areas where we are new enough that we don't know "the rules" and as such are not blinkered by them.

What the drafting table in Mycelium does is to provide a context for solving a problem. This provides a literal way of taking things outside "their proper place" by defining a new place for them.

Which points to the second element that is often overlooked in creativity: constraint.

We often think of creativity as being able to draw on any piece of knowledge in any situation in order to find the right solution to a problem. Indeed, we have been talking about it in exactly that way through much of this book. And in theory, that's right.

But in practical terms, we can all think of examples from our lives that show the weaknesses of this as a real world approach. Most of us will have gone to a restaurant, sat down to enjoy a meal, and opened the menu to see a hundred options all of which seem to blend into one. Or stood in front of a shelf filled with so many different versions of the same item that the sheer scope of choice is so overwhelming that we can't make any choice at all.

Sometimes the freedom to do anything, literally anything, is so overwhelming for brains that evolved to solve specific problems in specific contexts that we end up shutting down altogether.

By contrast, constraint can provide a focus that leads to creative problem solving. This is the root of the saying, "Necessity is the mother of invention." An example that springs to mind is the Apollo 13 space mission. When two of the craft's oxygen tanks failed and new procedures were needed that would bring the crew safely back to earth, they had no choice but to use what was there in the ship. The result is the stuff of legend and a major Hollywood film.

There is even a literary movement devoted to this principle that constraint fosters creativity. Oulipo arose out of the 1960s avant garde. At its core was the desire to find new ways to create literature. The tool used was the invention of new and imaginative forms of constraint, to see where they might lead. They led, among other things, to the writing of a 300 page novel (by George Perec, titled in English *A Void*) that doesn't contain the letter "e".

Adding an extra incentive (double points) for answers related to a specific category from the drafting table is a way of adding controlled constraint to the blend with Mycelium. As well as enhancing creativity through constraint, the provision of a third variable as a context in which the problem arises often provides the perfect recipe for the brain looking to grapple with a meaningful problem..

Let's go back to our worked example. When you add this extra element, your question is now something like:

"What would happen if ants and a glacier swapped places for a day...and double points if it involves reef ecosystems"

The mixture of total freedom to be creative, with a little bit of a restriction on the parameters of the problem, can really push you to an extra level of ingenuity. In the case of this question, my first thought is that one of the main threats to our reefs is the acidification of the ocean. And that ants produce formic acid.

One thing we might consider, for example, is how to find some way of hiving off the formic acid produced by ants and using it for some other purpose. Or devising some way of diverting water flows so that the bays into which glacial meltwater had flown are kept out of the same ocean current system as any reefs. Who knows, perhaps thinking like this might lead to some interesting thoughts about the actual problem of acidification.

You can see the benefit of having the slightly more complex question. The restraint forces you to think just that little bit harder. You can't settle on "the obvious" answers. Because there are no obvious answers.

But also, and in a similar vein, the extra item steers you just enough off the vast open spaces of being able to imagine anything and gives you a place to start. The problem with having the freedom to think of absolutely anything is that it's overwhelming. Sometimes so overwhelming that you end up falling back on familiarity. Whereas if you narrow the horizon a little you can end up in a far more interesting place. Narrow it too much, on the other hand, and you end up forcing the narrative.

But trying to connect two concrete objects or ideas in the context of a subject seems to provide a sweet spot. This formula of "joining two things in the context of a third" is something I have found over and over to be the goldilocks zone for creativity.

Mental hooks

We spent much of an earlier section looking at how to prime our mental archives so they find it easier to tease ideas from their "proper place." Now it's time to take that process one stage further.

We have so far spent this section looking at how to shape our mental tools so they are best equipped to form new things. Previous sections have looked at how to prepare our knowledge stores, as it were. We might think of this process as readying the ground to be mined, or even mining the ore. But we can go even further than priming our knowledge. That knowledge itself is made up of even smaller building blocks, and in this final section we will look at how to prepare those smallest building blocks to make them as reactive as possible, ready to explode into creative life.

Those elementary raw materials are the simple ideas themselves from which knowledge is constructed. Even the word idea is somewhat misleading as it suggests something quite complex. And what I am proposing here is to take something that is already simple, the mental equivalent of an atom, and break it into the smallest chunks possible, the subatomic particles of the mind. Being able to imagine an idea and break it down in this way will make the forming of fluid connections as effortless as it is possible to get.

Ideas like to have a place. In many ways they exist only in the context of a schema. "Dog" as an idea is only meaningful in the sense that people understand something by it. But to understand something by it is to think of it as having a place. Even if, across the whole of humanity, there are many different ideas of dog, each of them is nonetheless dependent for being understood on fitting somewhere.

But that fundamental property of ideas makes them hard to join up in creative new ways.

To make it easier to form those connections we need to loosen the bonds between ideas and their fixed places, to make them malleable. We need to be like s a smith heating iron in a forge, or a cook kneading then proving a dough, or an artist stretching and priming a canvas, or even a Lego fan arranging the pieces bag by bag before building.

To understand how we apply this process to ideas, making them malleable and pliant, let me use an example. It will help to show how ideas resist connection, and how to nudge them into more compliance until they actively seek it out.

Here is an example of a common creative thinking problem type:

"What would you get if you crossed a dog and a skyscraper?"

Start to answer the question.

As you do so, concentrate on what actually happens in your head when you read the question to yourself and think about how to tackle it. It's this self-observation that's key to understanding how ideas can "get in the way" of creativity for many people, and set us on the path to correcting the problem.

Mental imagery

At this point, I need to add an aside about mental imagery and aphantasia, which I mentioned when I talked about memory palaces.

Interestingly, when I teach creativity workshops, experience tells me at this point in proceedings, there is almost always someone who starts to look confused as I talk about mental pictures. Because, as they will often put it, "But when people say that, that's a metaphor. People don't *actually* see things in their head. Do they?"

It happens so regularly that now before I start this section, I tell people that they may be about to learn something about themselves. And it might feel as though it turns a part of their understanding of their identity and experience of the world on its head. And I signpost groups to places where they can find more information, like the Aphantasia Network[14].

Aphantasia simply means the absence of clear mental imagery. Like blindness, there are degrees, that range from blurred imagery or imagery with washed-out colours to no imagery at all. If you think that might apply to you, as it does to at least 3% of the population, the Aphantasia Network has some useful tests that will help you understand where your own imagery or absence of it falls on that line from clear through blurred to not there.

I also tell people that in my experience, people who are aphantasic find the technique I am about to describe a whole lot easier than people who have vivid mental imagery. Indeed I've found they often find it easier in general to form creative connections. Because in my experience mental imagery is one of people's key barriers to creative fluidity.

---

[14] https://aphantasia.com/

So what do I mean when I call mental imagery a barrier to creativity? After all, I've talked about memory palaces as a creative tool, and they rely on sensory imagination. What makes this internal sensory world a help in some circumstances and a hindrance in others?

Go back to the question in hand. "What would you get if you crossed a dog and a skyscraper?" And go back to your self-observation. Put what actually happens, in your head, in front of a lens. Imagine you are sitting watching your mind as if you were watching a screen. What exactly is playing on the screen in front of you when you read or hear the question?

What most commonly happens is this. When you read "dog" you might picture an actual dog. Maybe Hooch, the eponymous canine from the film Turner and Hooch, or Lassie, or a childhood pet. And then when you read "skyscraper" you might picture The Empire State Building, or The Shard, or the Burj el-Arab.

Our brains will regularly represent these more abstract notions like dog and skyscraper to us as a particular dog and a particular skyscraper in order to create a picture in our head. Many of us think through problems and scenarios by playing a movie in our heads. But when a movie plays, it does so with actual images, with a cast of specific characters and places and objects. And those turn an abstract or general question into something concrete and specific.

And when that happens the question:

"What would you get if you crossed a dog and a skyscraper?"

becomes:

"What do you get if you cross Lassie with the Burj el-Arab?"

New ideas just struggle to materialise at this point. You are stuck with a very particular realisation of a very particular image and once that happens, like the song goes, you just can't get it out of your head.

What we need is a way of enabling the brain swiftly and fluidly to move past this block (and it's the fact that aphantasic people are able to move straight to this stage that, in my experience, often enables them to form connections more fluidly; there are simply fewer steps in the process than there are for the rest of us).

To understand how to do this, let's go back to that riposte about mental imagery: "but isn't that a metaphor?" Because what we need to train our brains to do is, essentially, to get better at forming metaphors.

So what is a metaphor?

At its most basic, a metaphor is simply a way of talking about one thing in terms of another. The phrase "it's raining cats and dogs" is a metaphor. So is saying on a foggy day "it's a pea souper" (lots of metaphors seem to relate to weather – that could be a very British thing!).

What these examples show is that there is a further element. Metaphors replace something mundane or prosaic with something striking in order to bring an idea to life in the audience's minds. But it only works if the striking new idea has just the right amount of similarity to the original in just about the right respect to get our point across. Consider an example.

Imagine you are reporting on the qualifying stages of a sports competition. You are a reporter for the local paper of Snozzleborough United darts team. After years of languishing towards the lower end of the qualifying groups for the Snuffleshire darts open, the team has made good and won all 14 of their qualifying matches. Reaching for the mental thesaurus you type:

"Snozzleborough Steamrollers Snuffleshire Oppo to Reach First Final."

"Steamroller" is a word we see a lot in such writing. It may be teetering on the edge of cliché but many readers like it. It has oomph. Sometimes we see it taken a step further still: "Snozzleborough Juggernaut Steamrollers Through Snuffleshire Qualifiers," for example. We all know exactly what this means even though, literally, a juggernaut isn't going to steamroller anything.

We know that a darts team is not a piece of mechanical equipment designed to flatten out a surface. We know opposition teams are not things we should literally flatten in order to make them physically smooth so you can travel over the space they occupy more easily. In that respect it makes no "sense" to talk about a darts team "steamrollering" its opposition. And yet somehow the word conveys what we want to say so much better than simply saying, "Snozzleborough United had a very successful qualifying round, beating all of the opposing teams and qualifying for the final." And so the metaphor "steamroller" is in many ways "better" than a literal account. It conveys an additional layer of information to the simple facts.

So what does this have to do with forming more fluid connections?

If we think about what it is that makes metaphors work, it's the fact that at some level there is a point of connection between one thing and another thing. And that point of connection allows you to transfer a thought or an emotion that applies very powerfully to one of those objects and enable the other object to convey the same thought or emotion with equal power.

Those points of connection (in this case, the idea of overwhelming something that stands between you and something you want to do) are also the secret sauce in creativity. Isolating as many of them as possible within any given idea is the key to making the most connections of the broadest nature between that idea and any other.

The way we get around the block caused by mental imagery creates is to practise finding these points of connection in ideas. The easier it becomes to do this, the more of these points we will find when we need to. And the more we find, the more fluid our creativity can be.

These potential points of connection are the properties or fundamental elements of ideas, the subatomic particles that make up the atom of the idea. And they act rather like the hooks of velcro. Or the small sticky spines of a sundew. Or in a more sinister but perhaps familiar post-Covid image, the receptors on the shell of a virus. They just sit there, waiting, until they come into proximity of another idea at which point they latch onto its own hooks. And when they do latch together, those two ideas can become something original, interesting, meaningful.

Let's use our original question as a worked example of how to do this.

Let's start with the idea "dog". The process of finding connection points involves breaking it down into its properties systematically. To do that, we need a systematic way of proceeding.

Break that process down by looking, for any idea, at each of the following in order:

- **Properties** of the thing, both the things that come in through your **senses** ("red," or "smooth") and **scientific properties** (things such as "liquid" or "negative charge");
- **Personal associations**;
- **Word play,** whether that's puns, things that sound like something ("homophones") or things that look like something on paper ("homonyms");
- **Cultural associations**, including popular culture, creative arts, history, and more.

As you do this more you will develop your own categories alongside or instead of these.

So, how does this work for dogs and skyscrapers?

The process is rather like the inverse of the message we are meant to take away in the famous scene from Charles Dickens' *Hard Times* in which the soulless rote-teacher Gradgrind asks his class to describe a horse. The class dreamer, Sissy Jupe, is unable to answer his question. For her a horse is an image, the substance of dreams and imaginings, associations with the wildly romantic way of life of the circus she longs to join. When Gradgrind turns to his favourite, Bitzer, he gets the answer:

"Quadruped. Graminivorous. Forty teeth, namely twenty-four grinders, four eye-teeth, and twelve incisive. Sheds coat in the spring; in marshy countries, sheds hoofs, too. Hoofs hard, but requiring to be shod with iron. Age known by marks in mouth."

As readers we are meant to shake our heads in disapproval. But actually, while Sissy's imagined horse has some very handy personal associations, Bitzer's seemingly cold analysis is incredibly useful. This is exactly how we can break ideas down into their physical properties, and some of the more common behavioural traits.

So a dog's **properties** might include:

- Carnivorous
- Four legs
- Love jumping in water
- Love shaking themselves dry
- Furry
- Lots of different breeds
- Pedigree or mongrel distinction

- Tongues that tend to slobber
- Sticking their head out of the window of a car
- Fetching sticks

I'm sure you can think of many more. Give yourself ten minutes and see how many you can find.

The next heading, **personal associations**, is much more what Sissy had in mind. A dog to me is my childhood friend, but also the rather vicious creature that left my spouse traumatized during a trail race. It's every dog I've ever known, the smell of my parents' car after a day out in the mud, the comforting feeling of weight on my seven year-old legs from my granny's great dane who had forgotten he'd grown up, afternoons safe after school watching Deputy Dawg, the dachshund I imagine us walking on the Promenade des Anglais in our old age.

These are all vivid and powerful, and could well be the unique creative spark needed to unlock an idea. But that very intimacy also makes them hard to communicate. For that reason it's helpful to try and think beyond these very specific associations, using them as starting guns to fire you on countless other journeys, some of which you might share with others (like Sunday afternoons in your childhood spent on long walks with your family pet); some of which you could never begin to convey though they might lead you to common questions (why, for example, do some of us spend our lives chasing the same innocent happiness we felt on those Sunday afternoons?).

Word play is really interesting. It's both fun and a fascinating linguistic journey that can lead to wonderful insights into the world and history of cultures. It's also the moment, when I'm giving workshops, that I realise I might one day change this example to something other than "dog," especially when I've been encouraging people to shout out answers without inhibition. So I'll leave some things unsaid while making the point that where creativity is concerned, turning your censor off is vital, even if you can't always write them in a book which you would like families to be able to sit down and work through together.

Think just how many phrases and words there are that directly include the word "dog." There are obvious idioms like top dog and underdog (derived from ancient tree felling practice), words that originated with canines and came to have similar but different meanings like dog tags and doggie bags, there's the somewhat negative hang dog, dog tired, and dog days; the more positive dog's bollocks; and the absolutely slang like doggone, raining cats and dogs, and hotdogging. Then there are words and phrases that sort of incorporate the word even if it's not an obvious part of the meaning, like Dogger Bank and doggerel. There are also word plays with other languages. The Latin for dog is "canis," the root (pun intended) of canine teeth, the Canary Islands, and more recently made up words like canicross (humans running with dogs).

Cultural associations are by far the richest seam to mine, and another area where you can learn so much just from a very few moments looking at someone else's associations, together with a brief spell on a search engine or in conversation with ChatGPT.

To start, we have been talking so far about the relevance of different characters in Dickens' novel *Hard Times*, and although that hasn't been a discussion that's touched on dogs, it's the perfect example of a cultural association. And it also reminds me of another Dickens novel (and adaptation) which does contain a famous dog, *Oliver Twist*, and the villain Bill Sykes' sidekick Bullseye.

Take music as an example of the creative arts. For me associations encompass everything from Snoop Dogg and Who Let the Dogs Out to Suede's album Dog Man Star and the Michael Hutchence film Dogs in Space; the greyhounds on the iconic cover of Blur's Park Life to the dog-suited characters in Daft Punk's video of Around the World and the bizarre line from Prefab Sprout's King of Rock 'n' Roll, "hot dog, jumping frog, Albuquerque."

When it comes to dogs in film and TV, before you even start with everything from Huckleberry Hound to Lassie there's a whole website called Does The Dog Die where you can look up the fate of animals in works of culture so you avoid the fate of Phoebe in Friends watching Old Yeller only to get a nasty shock.

And sometimes there are multiple, interdisciplinary connections like the Scottish band Belle and Sebastian, named after the children's television series about a boy and his dog.

And if you look at internet memes it's like going deeper and deeper into a fractal. Just look at where you could end up if you started thinking too hard about all the associations of the crypto alt-coin Dogecoin, puffed and pumped by Elon Musk but which also sounds like it might be the private currency of the Venetian Doge.

That whirlwind tour barely scratches the surface (to show how rich a seam this can be, you may well have found yourself now primed so when you read the word "tour" you thought of a soldier's dog tags; and scratch may have given you an image of a dog, well, scratching). But even the opening section shows how useful a technique it can be when it comes to answering something like our original question.

Take those first properties.

- Carnivorous
- Four legs
- Love jumping in water
- Love shaking themselves dry
- Furry

If we take just a very few properties of skyscrapers, suddenly that velcro effect of hooks reaching out to clasp each other springs into action.

- Humans live inside
- Built on vast, solid foundations
- Covered in windows
- Kept stable by giant dampers
- Difficult to clean the windows

Skyscrapers are tall, made of metal, concrete, glass. They have lots of windows covering them, somewhat like the coat of fur on dogs. They need solid foundations and a really strong core running through them, like the paws and spine of a dog. They are full of rooms that are full of people, the same way a stomach might be full of meat.

It's the similarity of those properties which provide the potential links, the hooks finding each other and connecting.

The rooms/stomach connection, combined with "carnivorous," could lead you to imagining some kind of sinister plot from some faceless corporate evil mastermind to disguise tower blocks as cute puppies only to have them devour you as soon as you walk inside.

A workshop I ran once came up with a great windows/fur idea, solving the problem of how you wash the windows on a skyscraper by imagining it shaking itself clean like a dog that's been rolling in mud. You could even take it further, having the giant dog that shakes the windows dry use that ability to create a shaking motion to act as the building's damper.

Exercise 14: Walking the Dog

If you really want to see just how many concepts cluster around a single word (each one of those the gateway to many possible creative associations), start a journal of associations, just with the word dog, in a notebook or on an app and carry it around with you everywhere for a week. Stop every time you think of something and write it down. Keep writing until the new associations dry up.

And at the end of the week, see just how many you have.

You can spend as long as you want breaking down any single idea in this way. You can even create whole project files and keep returning to them. In fact, I would suggest that for at least one idea you do exactly that, for at least a week, spending time every day revisiting it. That will give you a picture of just how vast the network of properties of every single idea in your head actually is.

But it's even more important to get used to the habit of doing this. That way it will become second nature, and every time you learn something new you will, quite literally, see it in a very different light.

I call this process of idea disentangling arpeggiation, which is a term musicians will be familiar with. Arpeggio, and the verb arpeggiate that comes from it, refers to a way of playing a chord so that, instead of playing all the notes that make up the chord together, producing the familiar single blend of sound, each individual note is played separately, in sequence.

You could also think of it a bit like those deconstructed pies that were all the rage in fancy restaurants a year or so ago.

The principle is the same. The idea of a thing, the atom, is like a chord. What gives it its special character is the particular arrangement of all its myriad (and often personal to everyone, hence no two people ever truly have the same idea) individual elements: the notes, the subatomic particles.

And just as one note can form a part of many chords (and one ingredient can form part of many pies) so each of the elements you identify could form part of many different ideas. It might work slightly differently for properties like "has four legs" from cultural or personal associations. In the former case, many things might have four legs. In the latter case, it will be more like metaphors, creating the same feelings or memories or fulfilling a similar need. But in all cases, it is the way the ingredients of ideas can come together to form something new that functions as the creative secret sauce.

This technique is something you can practise at your desk. I use the backs of old sheets of A4 because I want to have more space than a notebook will give me. And then I file the sheets away and from time to time get them out and look through two different ones at random to see where they intersect and where those intersections might take me. It's something you can do in your head as you walk down the street, maybe with something you stumble across, or something you find in a shop window, putting things into a voice note or a pocketbook or a note to yourself on your phone as you go. Or you can use a digital tool like Notion or Evernote and let the software start forming its own links.

Living Creatively

In the words of one of my favourite poets, Vanessa Kisuule, "You've made it this far. Remember that.[15]"The hard work, the history, and the heavy theory are behind you. In this last section I want to offer just a few suggestions on what, actually, is the hardest part of all for most people. And that is actually adding creativity to your life, whether that's the techniques outlined here, or simply thinking about things differently from how you have done before.

Because exercises work well on the pages of a book. And they fit very nicely into a certain kind of life. Or a lab. Or a university. Or a think tank or tech job or corporation or government body where your job is to do new things.

But those settings are a luxury most people don't have. You are probably reading this book because you don't have a life with hours a day to spare or an environment filled with people encouraging and empowering you to think differently (no, the Apple advert doesn't count). You probably wish you could spend hours doing everything in this book but know family, friends, the necessities of rent and food, caring, building a healthy body to house the mind you long to be healthy too: all these things mean you just don't have those hours.

In the previous book in this series, *Living in Longhand*, I talk a lot about how to fit different parts of your life and your dreams together into a jigsaw that at least kind of functions, most of the time, and allows you to keep alive both hope and necessity. I hope you'll read it!

This section isn't intended as an exhaustive exploration of time management or goal setting. It's based on some simple ideas:

---

[15] https://www.youtube.com/watch?v=3b-B4G8IQdk

- that doing something is better than doing nothing. And that doing a tiny amount regularly will add up over time. So it outlines ways in which you can do small things when you have small amounts of time.

- That for some people, the thing holding them back is not quite knowing how to start or feeling a kind of "blank page fear," not being able to take the first step because that feels like something huge. For those people, this section has some first steps that, I hope, won't feel huge.

- That you can build creativity into other activities (just like we talked about with extracting value from boring tasks). That actually, building creativity into other things is in itself a creative act. It is connecting two previously unconnected things. I'll end this section with a few ways to combine creative practice with something else, maximising the difference you can make to your life from a single activity (and sometimes providing a level of stimulus to your rain that can be way bigger than the sum of the parts!)

Creative walking

I won't rehash the anecdotes you undoubtedly already know from YouTube videos and Reddit. Many famous people through history have used walking to come up with their ideas. And no, it's not an urban legend or confirmation bias: there's some actual evidence that walking does indeed improve creativity[16]. We'll take all that for granted. If you can, go for walks. It's good for creativity and problem solving: my spouse and I think through all our major decisions together on walks that take up many hours. It's also, when done by the right person in the right circumstance, good for general health.

This is not about the what (walking) or the why (it's great for many things) but the how. How do you get the most creative benefit from a walk?

If you want to immerse yourself in a big problem without interruption, then ignore what I am about to say, which is more about walking as a general practice and training technique. Also, walk somewhere you know really well that has even terrain and no busy road crossings!

As I hinted in the last section, take something with you that will enable you to note things down as you think of them. Ideas on walks can be ephemeral and evasive. What might seem vivid at the time has a nasty habit of fading the moment you get home and sit down. I use a Rite in the Rain notebook and a Fisher Space Pen because I live in England and if I only went out for walks when it wasn't wet I would spend months at a time indoors.

One way of making good use of walks is to create specific maps.

---

[16] https://news.stanford.edu/2014/04/24/walking-vs-sitting-042414/

Before you set out for a walk, think of a single thing you might come across fairly regularly on a walk, and set out to create a map of everywhere you come across examples of it. That might be something like "has needles" to take a very obvious example. As you walk (you could use a camera if you want), note down every time you see something with needles. Try to find as many **different** kinds of needle as possible. So things that have needles might not just be conifers, but hospitals, or even offices where people "needle" each other.

Another one might be "spikes," which could apply to thorny plants, or fences, spires on churches or even venues like stadiums that have a spike in attendance on certain days.

Technology allows you to tag locations on digital maps and create virtual, themed spaces that you can share with others. I find the potential for what augmented reality could do for creativity and building new ideas incredibly exciting.

Or you can simply draw a map when you get home, slowly making a whole book full of maps of the same space seen through different lenses. It's not only a great way of making connections between places and things that would otherwise seem disparate and unconnected. It's also a great way of experiencing the same place in different ways, of making the familiar unfamiliar as the saying goes. And that's a great habit to carry over to the rest of life.

And of course, we already know that navigating is incredibly good for your creative brain. Orienteering (navigating between checkpoints) is a wonderful exercise, and you can create your own routes for your walks, studying them in advance and deciding on points you need to pass through, and the order to pass through them, figuring out how you will steer your course and then following those mental instructions on your actual walk. This, needless to say, is also a great way to start building memory journeys–you could even walk down an existing memory journey and pay attention to the pieces of knowledge you have mentally planted along the route as you go.

Observing and questioning

You can enhance the quality of work you put into the techniques we have studied in this book is to practise the basic elements of those techniques in daily life.

One way to do this is to practise using your senses in a really focused way. Most people have a lot of sensory filters. When they walk down a street, their ears, eyes, and noses are assaulted by inputs coming from all sides. At any moment we could be passing many different conversations, the sounds from ten or more car engines, trees full of birds, more than one tune or bass line from music playing out of a window, several sets of trolley wheels grinding on concrete, and countless shoes hitting pavement. Yet most people can still have a conversation with the person they're walking with and only hear what that person is saying. Not because their ears aren't picking up the other sounds, but because their brains are filtering them out to tune into the one sound it really wants to concentrate on.

One reason autistic people get overloaded by sensory input is that their brains don't fully carry out this filtering. So just walking down the street can mean hearing every single one of those things, individually, all the time. It's no wonder we get so utterly exhausted and can feel an overwhelming need to get out of the hecticness and hide in a dark silent room!

For people whose sensory filters keep things out so much of the time, focusing on switching them off for a while and really concentrating on picking out each individual sound or smell (smell is a powerful sense, but obviously be careful with this one: the world we live in, especially our urban areas, is full of toxins you really don't want to lean in and fill your lungs with), every word on the signs around us, the individual leaves on trees, cracks in the pavement, even separate blades of grass.

This is, of course, a form of mindfulness. Mindfulness centres on noticing things in the present moment in as much clarity and as wholly as you can. And while a tiny section of a book on creativity isn't the place to get into a discussion of mindfulness as a practice, if you are interested in thinking around it, I highly recommend memory expert Anthony Metivier's many YouTube videos on the way mindfulness can benefit memory and how memory techniques function as a form of mindfulness[17].

For now, we will simply note that practising the observance of individual sensations can greatly enhance techniques such as the memory palace (by filling it with different fragrances), and the ability to break down ideas more fully into their constituents (for example, by distinguishing every kind of noise a dog can make, and in which contexts).

Questioning plays a similar role to observation in sharpening our skills. It attunes us to the possibility that things could be another way, shaking things slightly loose from their "proper place." And, like observation, adding questioning to our daily lives will make it easier to do when we are faced with a crucial or urgent problem that needs our attention.

Questioning can be very specifically based on the techniques we have already looked at. You can carry the 10 questions for interrogating a subject with you everywhere you go and apply one or more to the things you encounter as you go about your day.

Or you can combine questioning with observation: "How many trees are there on this road?", "Do I hear more different bird songs in the morning or the evening?", "What is the most common type of shop in my home town?"

And you can dig around (separate from anything that requires a project all of its own) with some research. Maybe ask yourself "Why?" about something you had taken for granted at least once a week. "Why is a double yellow line used as a symbol to mean no parking?", "Why is it normal for people to have cereal for breakfast but not lunch?

---

[17] For example https://www.youtube.com/watch?v=uAz3_pkqXqc

Play

It would be tempting to approach many of the techniques outlined in this book as though they were tasks, assignments, or processes to master. That's never the way I'd choose to tackle creativity. One of the keys to being creative, like so many areas in life, is playing.

Play matters to creativity for many reasons. When we play is when we find it easiest to switch off our filters and self-censors. Or, rather, when we most often find ourselves ignoring them and just going where the moment takes us. That state of unconscious flow is pretty much a defining characteristic of both creativity and of play.

It's also when we play that we most easily allow ourselves to get delighted by things that are, taken in their literal sense, utterly absurd. Think of almost any game, with its layer of complex rules, conventions, and history. The leg before wicket rule in cricket or the artificial bids in bridge to which we literally give the name "conventions" or the "miss" rule in snooker, when we take a step back, are meaningless inventions. And yet people commit themselves with every last drop of their passion to debating them as though they were the answer to food scarcity. And it's that ability to suspend disbelief and commit to the absurd as though life depends on it that makes games so useful. As well as such fun. Because on a different, er, playing field that ability to commit to an idea utterly outside our experience is something our lives might just depend on.

I realise that telling someone to have fun is a strategy that has a minimal chance of success at best. Organised fun sends the kind of shiver and incomprehension through me as architects designing research facilities who talk about planned spontaneity.

So instead of simply saying, "Play!" I simply want to encourage you to adopt a playful mindset. As an extension of observing and questioning. Within the bounds of the law and avoiding being a public nuisance, the parameters of consensual relationships and healthful living, and financial security: Do naughty things. Do things you shouldn't. Do things people you know would disapprove of. Do things that make you find yourself saying, "I really shouldn't!"

What I really mean is: write in the margins of your books (and dog ear the pages); tell people you don't want to see that you've got a really important meeting and bunk off to the cinema; eat roast potatoes with a spoon; wear a saucepan as a hot; take a (broken, lost, not in use) traffic cone home and plant potatoes in it.

There's a famous exchange in *Alice's Adventures in Wonderland*:

> Alice laughed. 'There's no use trying,' she said. 'One can't believe impossible things.'
>
> 'I daresay you haven't had much practice,' said the Queen. 'When I was your age, I always did it for half-an-hour a day. Why, sometimes I've believed as many as six impossible things before breakfast."

Make having that approach to the world a life goal.

- Commit to something absurd for no meaningful reason;
- Lose yourself in the moment;
- Find delight in something that has absolutely no practical use.

And if you can do each of these things every day so much the better.

And when you find yourself enjoying something you do, something impractical or without moral or social benefit, something that's not nourishing or growth-creating or widely valued, and you find yourself realising this, try to develop a practice of noticing that realisation, shrug your shoulders, say "**** it!" and carry on without guilt.

Combine things that aren't usually combined

It was inevitable that this should be the final, crowning thing on my list for creative living. Combining things that aren't usually combined and seem to make no sense together is the essence of creativity. Doing it in your day to day life is also a form of play. And because it's unfamiliar, it's always going to require deliberate practice as you teach your mind and body to make shapes and patterns and movements they have never made before, and sharp observation along with questioning, "How can I do this better? How can I make the transitions and connections more seamless? The experience more integrated?"

In *Living in Longhand* I talked at great length about hybrid training, which has become increasingly popular, in which people train two or more things that have no obvious link to each other, and a seemingly obvious contraindication. Like endurance running and powerlifting. Or memorisation and rowing.

Usually hybrid training means dividing your week or month or training block up so that you can do sessions related to each of the different elements you are training.

But what if you actually combined them? Until I wondered about the possibility, I had no idea that there is a whole formal set-up dedicated to "chess boxing." I was, however, already aware of the existence of diving chess, which has long been part of the Mind Sports Olympiad.

Value extraction is one way you can combine two things. Though combining two things, both of which you enjoy, is even better. As a performance poet, I've been delighted over the years to find out just how many subjects of study have their own take on the poetry slam. At the University of Oxford we even had a Science Poetry network for several years.

Orienteering, which we've already mentioned, is another great way to combine very different skills. And many martial arts grew out of exactly this kind of desire to combine physical control with mental focus.

I've spent many years trying to combine activities into challenges that are fun, unusual, and stimulating. By and large these have been activities done in sequence. I celebrated being 50, for example, by rowing 2000 metres as fast as I could, doing the 3 conventional power lifts, memorising a deck of cards, solving a Rubik's cube, doing a creativity challenge and then running 50 kilometres. It was everything I wanted it to be. But I did each activity in sequence, not in parallel.

One of the things I've found that does genuinely combine activities is cube running. Which is exactly what it sounds like. Solving a Rubik's cube while running. As I have said before, this is best done on very even ground with no road crossings (ideally on a track). When I came back from the first attempt at doing it, I had no idea it was a thing other people did. But it turns out there are even official records, for things like most cubes solved while running a marathon.

I am delighted you have made it this far. Let me indulge in one of my favourite pastimes, the historical misquote. This book, its exercises and its discoveries, are not the glorious near vertical off-piste slopes down which your brain can carve a trial. They are not the black runs that hone your craft for those life-changing, powder-skimming runs. But they are, perhaps, the first baby steps to the ski lift that will carry you to the nursery slopes that will prepare you to begin to hone your creative craft as you set out on the adventure that will last a lifetime.

Buckle in, and in the next book in this series we will look at the ingredient without which creativity can become just a fun workout for the brain: communication, the key to turning ideas into impact.

If you have enjoyed this book or found it in some way useful, please do leave a review and let your friends know.

Dan Holloway

Acknowledgements

As far back as I can remember, to quote the first movie I saw at the main cinema in Oxford when I arrived here as a student, I always wanted to be a creator.

These people who made that happen, the Pesci and De Niro of the creative world as it were, are the poor souls saddled with the responsibility of birthing this sprawling thicket of words.

I can only pick out a few of the players. To attempt to make the list exhaustive would be to set myself up never to finish this book for fear of omission. My sincerest apologies to any I have missed. More sincere apologies still to those I have named: what an awful thing it is to bear the burden of having a named part in such a farce.

At the very earliest stage, Hazel Cole who encouraged me to pursue my love of words, and Bill Church who lit the fire under my love of numbers. What you see before you is the chimaera of their making.

As a fragile teenager seeking solace from schoolyard bullies and the rain alike, I found myself one day in the school bridge club run by Andrew Kambites. I had no idea at the time what a legend of the game he was (and still is), but the passion he gave me for this remarkable game transformed my life in so many ways.

As a graduate student I fell under the very different but eerily similar spells of Bill Hartston and Martha Nussbaum. Bill had been a childhood hero thanks to TV chess. I rediscovered him through his newspaper column on creativity. Since 1997 I am delighted to have known him personally, meeting up once a year at the Mind Sports Olympiad. His words to me in the competitions first year, "you have a very sick mind," provided all the encouragement I needed to fuel my creative journey ever since. Martha's Ascents of Love Lecture Series the same year showed me what was possible when you give disciplinary boundaries over to their natural porosity. More than two decade later I had the privilege of asking the first question when she gave her acceptance lecture for the Kyoto Prize. A brilliant scholar and a fellow runner, her life is a template for my aspirations.

Communicating was, of course, my first love. For a glorious decade as a performance poet and novelist I surrounded myself with some of the brightest most dazzling lights I have ever known: all the glorious collaborators at Year Zero, Not the Oxford Literary Festival, eight cuts gallery, and The New Libertines: we had joy, we had fun, we had winters in magnificent darkness.

There are too many creative inspirations for naming to be fair. But those whose lines run deepest through this book are Katelan Foisy, Orna Ross, Joanna Penn, Veronika von Volkova, Rohan Quine, Tom de Freston, Kiran Millwood Hargrave, Claire Trevien, and Cameron Chapman. Of course, without Dennis, the Albion Beatnik Bookstore, and all that happened there, above ground and below, from my first book launch to the Great Jericho Poetry Brawl; gigs, galleries, manifestos, and the scattering of ashes; I would never have emerged from the chrysalis. Most, and always, the late, great Davy Mac of the aforementioned ashes, such a quiet looking soul in your hat and waistcoat, when you opened your mouth you spat fire and perfume across the ether.

Mark Mann: you believed in my daft ideas when no one else did. Vicky McGuinness: you gave me opportunities when no one else would. Aditi Lahiri: you literally saved my life.

Sarm Derbois, Emma Charleston, Sophie Tallis, and Alessandro Vatri. Mycelium would not exist without you. Mirela Zaneva: reading your remarkable answers the very first time I demonstrated Mycelium, at the Natural History Museum, was the moment I knew I was doing what I had to do. Your subsequent victory at the Creative Thinking World Championships meant far more than my own. Mo Schoenfeld: your belief and support in what I have been doing sustained me through so many moments of doubt. Thank you.

I am indebted to my incredible cover designer Jane Dixon-Smith for her ability to fight her way through my jumbled mood boards to get to the hidden idea in my head. To Yunseo Cho, student at the Ruskin School of Fine Art, whose patience with a hyperactive subject delivered a photoshoot I am thrilled by. To Camilla Rock and Richard Auburn whose administrative acumen and breathtaking patience have so often enabled me to do what I do least worst. To Sam Warburton, who undertook the daunting task of setting my words to her incredible art with remarkable grace and skill. And of course to Veronika von Volkova in whose remarkable images you could lose yourself forever.

Most of the ideas in this book germinated, took form, and became practically applicable during the endless long walks with my spouse that are an integral part of our ideal lives. Their wit, ingenuity, and unique ways of understanding the world never cease to amaze and delight me. Anything truly insightful or original is theirs. Anything incompletely articulated or insufficiently useful is mine.

Printed in Great Britain
by Amazon